مسائل الجاهلية

ASPECTS OF THE DAYS OF IGNORANCE

لشيخ الإسلام محمد بن عبد الوهاب رحمه الله

BY SHAYKH AL-ISLAM MUHAMMAD IBN 'ABDIL-WAHHAAB

WORKBOOK
PREPARED BY
MOOSAA RICHARDSON

Limited license to print in November 2019 granted to Germantown Masjid (*Masjid as-Sunnah an-Nabawiyyah*) in Germantown, Philadelphia (USA).

First Print Edition: Rabee' al-Awwal 1441 (November 2019)

Aspects of the Days of Ignorance, Workbook for Germantown Masjid's Winter Seminar (2019) / Author: Shaykh al-Islam Muhammad ibn 'Abdil-Wahhaab / Translator: Moosaa Richardson / Proofreader: Anwar Wright / Cover design: Awal Studio.

ISBN 978-1708514037

1. Nonfiction —Religion —Islam —Theology.

2. Education & Reference —Foreign Language Study —Arabic.

TABLE OF CONTENTS

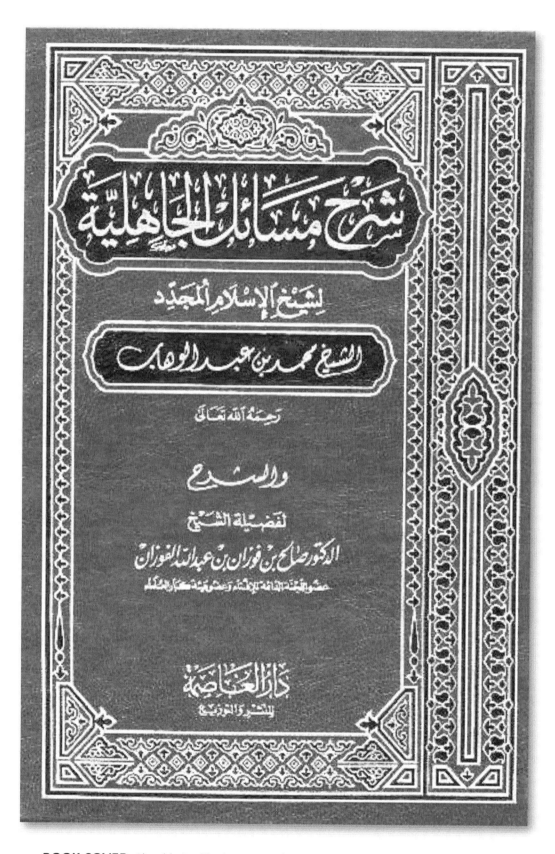

شرح مسائل الجاهلية

لشيخ الإسلام المجدد

الشيخ محمد بن عبد الوهاب

رحمه الله تعالى

والشرح

لفضيلة الشيخ

الدكتور صالح بن فوزان بن عبد الله الفوزان

عضو الهيئة الدائمة للإفتاء وعضو هيئة كبار العلماء

دار العباضة
للنشر والتوزيع

BOOK COVER: Shaykh Saalih al-Fowzaan's explanation of *Masaa'il al-Jaahiliyyah*.

ABOUT THIS WORKBOOK

All praise is due to Allah, the Lord, Creator, and Sustainer of all things. May He raise the rank of and grant peace to His Prophet and final Messenger, Muhammad, and all of his respected family and noble companions.

Our Magnificent and Ever Generous Creator has bestowed upon us every type of favor and blessing, the greatest of which is His Guidance to the true Religion of submission to Him Alone in worship, the Religion of Islam.

﴿فَمَن يُرِدِ ٱللَّهُ أَن يَهْدِيَهُ يَشْرَحْ صَدْرَهُ لِلْإِسْلَٰمِ﴾

"Whomever Allah wants to guide, He opens his chest up to Islam." [6:125]

In order to truly appreciate this great blessing, one must look back and reflect about what he was upon before guidance reached him. Allah reminds us:

﴿وَكُنتُمْ عَلَىٰ شَفَا حُفْرَةٍ مِّنَ ٱلنَّارِ فَأَنقَذَكُم مِّنْهَا﴾

"You were right at the brink of a pit of Fire, and He saved you from it." [3:103]

The exemplary gratitude of the noble Companions of the Messenger of Allah (may Allah raise his rank and grant him peace) and the great value they attached to Allah's guidance led them to look back in appreciation and look forward with concern. Take, for instance, the famous question of Huthayfah ibn al-Yamaan (may Allah be pleased with him:

"إِنَّا كُنَّا فِي جَاهِلِيَّةٍ وَشَرٍّ، فَجَاءَنَا اللهُ بِهَذَا الخَيْرِ، فَهَلْ بَعْدَ هَذَا الخَيْرِ شَرٌّ؟"

"We used to be in *Jaahiliyyah* and evil, and then Allah brought us this goodness. But will there be any evil after this goodness?"[1]

So, as we look back in appreciation, and as we look forward in worry and concern, it is also important to note that we need to learn about all traits of *Jaahiliyyah*, even those we were not specifically guilty of, in order to properly learn our Religion and stay clear of all prohibited matters. Allah, the Exalted and Majestic, has commanded the believing women:

﴿وَلَا تَبَرَّجْنَ تَبَرُّجَ ٱلْجَٰهِلِيَّةِ ٱلْأُولَىٰ﴾

"And do not come out improperly dressed, with the open display of the first era of *Jaahiliyyah*." [33:33]

---

[1] *Saheeh al-Bukhaaree* (no. 3606, 7084), *Saheeh Muslim* (no. 1847)

And the Messenger of Allah (may Allah raise his rank and grant him peace) once rebuked a Companion for uttering a displeasing word from the speech of *Jaahiliyyah*, saying:

$$\text{«إِنَّكَ امْرُؤٌ فِيكَ جَاهِلِيَّةٌ!»}$$

"You are a man who [still] **has** [some] ***Jaahiliyyah* within him!"**[2]

Based on that, we can summarize our intention in studying this topic:

- To appreciate Allah's Guidance, in comparison to the *Jaahiliyyah* we were upon
- To remain vigilant against returning to familiar traits of *Jaahiliyyah*
- To learn about all other traits of *Jaahiliyyah* and avoid them as well

We ask our Lord to honor us with the distinction He grants His truly believing servants, the upright people of sincerity, faith, and righteousness, and that He distances us from all blameworthy traits of *Jaahiliyyah*.

This book, *Masaa'il al-Jaahiliyyah* (*Aspects of the Days of Ignorance*), is a unique and powerfully insightful work serving this important topic, authored by one of the most knowledgeable and authoritative scholars of the past few centuries, Shaykh al-Islam Muhammad ibn 'Abdil-Wahhaab at-Tameemee (may Allah have Mercy on him).

About this book, Shaykh Saalih ibn 'Abdil-'Azeez Aal ash-Shaykh (may Allah preserve him) said:

> These issues are extremely important in our lives today. The callers to Allah, the Mighty and Majestic, should be utilizing them and explaining them in their study circles and in their propagation of the Religion. When people hear that certain things are from the behavioral trends of the Jews, or the people of *Jaahiliyyah*, along with textual proof of that and the explanations of the people of knowledge, and that these things are still found amongst this *Ummah*, it acts as one of the most beneficial approaches in the propagation of Islam, one of the praiseworthy Salafee methods in *da'wah*... These are tremendous points which, no doubt, we are in need of in every time, and especially in this time. Reviewing them and reminding the people about them is a necessity.[3]

Our brother, Ustaadh Hassan Somali (may Allah preserve him), and the community of *Masjid as-Sunnah an-Nabawiyyah* in Germantown, Philadelphia, have done well in selecting this book for this year's winter seminar. I, personally, am humbled and honored that he and his community have entrusted me with the preparation of this workbook for the classes. I ask Allah to grant us all success, and to bless all of the scholars, students of knowledge, organizers, attendees, and supporters involved, and to make our cooperation a source of joy for us the Day we meet Him.

In this workbook, you will find the original Arabic text of the book, *Masaa'il al-Jaahiliyyah*, paired with my translation of it into English, with ample space to take notes for each point. Appendices in the back provide a chain of transmission for the text, the complete, uninterrupted text of the English translation, and the fully voweled Arabic text of the book as well.

You will also find a total of 12 quizzes to challenge your understanding and memorization of this important text. Five daily quizzes with multiple choice questions have been prepared to check your

---

[2] *Saheeh al-Bukhaaree* (no. 30, 6050), *Saheeh Muslim* (no. 1661). See: Aspect #95, p.102.
[3] From his classes explaining *Masaa'il al-Jaahiliyyah* (p.1, slightly adapted), as found on his official website at this link: https://www.saleh.af.org.sa/sites/default/files/books/023.pdf (Accessed: November 15, 2019).

understanding of the lessons of each of the five days of the seminar. A 25-question mastery test awaits you once you have studied the entire book and reviewed the five quizzes. For more advanced students who choose to memorize the Arabic text along with its study, five more daily quizzes and another comprehensive test are also included.[4]

Beyond this winter's lessons, students are further encouraged to review this text by committing to an even more dedicated study, using one of the [Arabic] explanations of the following scholars:

- Shaykh Mahmood al-Aaloosee [d.1270], may Allah have Mercy on him [printed]
- Shaykh Zayd al-Madkhalee [d.1435], may Allah have Mercy on him [printed]
- Shaykh Saalih al-Fowzaan, may Allah preserve him [printed]
- Shaykh Saalih ibn 'Abdil-'Azeez Aal ash-Shaykh, may Allah preserve him [recordings]
- Shaykh 'Abdur-Razzaaq al-Badr, may Allah preserve him [recordings]

In the English Language, perhaps there may be some benefit in reviewing a set of freely available recordings hosted by our brothers at TROID (www.TROID.org). These classes were readings from the printed explanation of Shaykh Saalih al-Fowzaan (may Allah preserve him). By the Permission of Allah, and success is only through Him, the book was completed in 39 sessions in the year 1434.

I ask Allah that He grant me and you success in attaining His Pleasure and in drawing near to Him. May He -the Exalted and Most High- raise the rank of Muhammad and grant him and his family and companions an abundance of peace.

ABUL-'ABBAAS

MOOSAA RICHARDSON
Education Director
First Muslim Mosque
Pittsburgh, Pennsylvania
Email: MR@bakkah.net
Twitter: @1MMeducation

---

[4] There are some minor differences between some of the printings of the books, *Masaa'il al-Jaahiliyyah*. The text used for this workbook is intended to match, for the most part, the printing used in Shaykh Saalih al-Fowzaan's explanation.

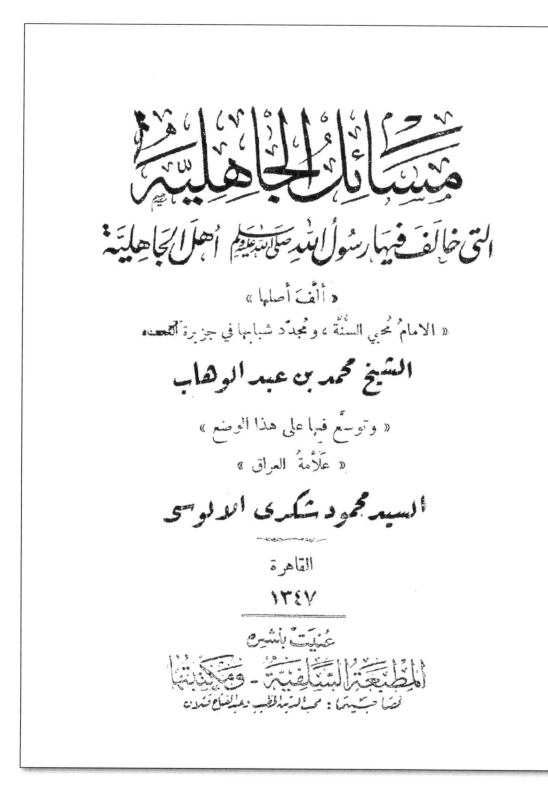

مسائل الجاهلية

التي خالف فيها رسول الله صلى الله عليه وسلم أهل الجاهلية

« ألّف أصلها »

« الامام مُحيي السُّنة ، ومجدّد شبابها في جزيرة العرب »

الشيخ محمد بن عبد الوهاب

« وتوسّع فيها على هذا الوضع »

« علّامة العراق »

السيد محمود شكري الآلوسي

القاهرة

١٣٤٧

عُنيت بنشر

المطبعة السلفية ـ ومكتبتها

An old Egyptian printing, nearly a century old, of Shaykh Mahmood al-Aaloosee's explanation of *Masaa'il al-Jaahiliyyah*. (May Allah have Mercy on him.)

INTRODUCTION

The Text, the Author, and the Topic

IN THE NAME OF ALLAH, THE MOST GRACIOUS, THE EVER-MERCIFUL

هَذِهِ أُمُورٌ خَالَفَ فِيهَا رَسُولُ اللهِ صَلَّى اللهُ عَلَيْهِ وَسَلَّمَ أَهْلَ الْجَاهِلِيَّةِ الْكِتَابِيِّينَ وَالأُمِّيِّينَ، مِمَّا لَا غِنَى لِلْمُسْلِمِ عَنْ مَعْرِفَتِهِ.

فَالضِّدُّ يُظْهِرُ حُسْنَهُ الضِّدُّ   وَبِضِدِّهَا تَتَبَيَّنُ الأَشْيَاءُ

These are affairs in which the Messenger of Allah -may Allah raise his rank and grant him peace- opposed the people of Jaahiliyyah, the People of Scripture, as well as the illiterate people [with no book]. These affairs are absolutely necessary for every Muslim to know about.

An opposite highlights the good of its counterpart,
        As by way of their opposites, things are made clear.

DISBELIEF

THE MOST DANGEROUS ASPECT OF JAAHILIYYAH

فَأَهَمُّ مَا فِيهَا وَأَشَدُّهَا خَطَرًا: عَدَمُ إِيْمَانِ الْقَلْبِ بِمَا جَاءَ بِهِ الرَّسُولُ صَلَّى اللهُ عَلَيْهِ وَسَلَّمَ، فَإِنِ انْضَافَ إِلَى ذَلِكَ اسْتِحْسَانُ مَا عَلَيْهِ أَهْلُ الْجَاهِلِيَّةِ، تَمَّتِ الْخَسَارَةُ، كَمَا قَالَ تَعَالَـــــــى: ﴿ وَٱلَّذِينَ ءَامَنُواْ بِٱلْبَٰطِلِ وَكَفَرُواْ بِٱللَّهِ أُوْلَـٰٓئِكَ هُمُ ٱلْخَٰسِرُونَ ﴾ [العنكبوت: ٥٢].

The most crucial and severely dangerous of that is the lack of heart-based faith in what the Messenger came with, may Allah raise his rank and grant him peace. When that is coupled with admiration of the what the people of Jaahiliyyah are/were upon, it is then a complete loss, as He, the Most High, says, "Those who believe in falsehood and disbelieve in Allah, such are the true losers." [29:52]

ASPECT 1

CALLING UPON SAINTS FOR THEIR INTERCESSION

الْمَسْأَلَةُ الْأُولَى: أَنَّهُمْ يَتَعَبَّدُونَ بِإِشْرَاكِ الصَّالِحِينَ فِي دُعَاءِ اللهِ وَعِبَادَتِهِ، يُرِيدُونَ

شَفَاعَتَهُمْ عِنْدَ اللهِ لِظَنِّهِمْ أَنَّ اللهَ يُحِبُّ ذَلِكَ، وَأَنَّ الصَّالِحِينَ يُحِبُّونَهُ، كَمَا قَالَ

تَعَالَــــى: ﴿ وَيَعْبُدُونَ مِن دُونِ ٱللَّهِ مَا لَا يَضُرُّهُمْ وَلَا يَنفَعُهُمْ وَيَقُولُونَ هَٰؤُلَآءِ

شُفَعَٰٓؤُنَا عِندَ ٱللَّهِ ﴾ [يونس: ١٨]، وَقَالَ تَعَالَــــى: ﴿ وَٱلَّذِينَ ٱتَّخَذُواْ مِن دُونِهِۦٓ

أَوْلِيَآءَ مَا نَعْبُدُهُمْ إِلَّا لِيُقَرِّبُونَآ إِلَى ٱللَّهِ زُلْفَىٰٓ ﴾ [الزمر: ٣].

THE FIRST ASPECT: In their worship, they would direct a share of their supplications and other rites to righteous people (saints), while that was to be for Allah alone. They assumed that such people could intercede for them in front of Allah, and that Allah loved that, and that the righteous also loved that, as He, the Most High, says, "They worship those beside Allah who do not harm them, nor benefit them, saying: These are our intercessors with Allah." [10:18] He, the Most High, also says, "And those who take protectors besides Allah [say]: We do not worship them except that they bring us closer to Allah." [39:3]

ASPECT 1

THE MOST CRUCIAL POINT OF OPPOSITION

وَهَذِهِ أَعْظَمُ مَسْأَلَةٍ خَالَفَهُمْ فِيهَا رَسُولُ اللهِ صَلَّى اللهُ عَلَيْهِ وَسَلَّمَ، فَأَتَى بِالْإِخْلَاصِ، وَأَخْبَرَ أَنَّهُ دِينُ اللهِ الَّذِي أَرْسَلَ بِهِ جَمِيعَ الرُّسُلِ، وَأَنَّهُ لَا يُقْبَلُ مِنَ الْأَعْمَالِ إِلَّا الْخَالِصُ، وَأَخْبَرَ أَنَّ مَنْ فَعَلَ مَا اسْتَحْسَنُوا فَقَدْ حَرَّمَ اللهُ عَلَيْهِ الجَنَّةَ وَمَأْوَاهُ النَّارُ.

This is the greatest issue the Messenger of Allah opposed them in, may Allah raise his rank and grant him peace. In contrast, he came with true sincerity [of Monotheistic worship], and he informed them that this was the true Religion of Allah with which He had sent all Messengers. No deed would ever be accepted, except one done sincerely [for Allah alone]. Additionally, he informed them that whoever did whatever they deemed to be correct (i.e. polytheism) would be barred by Allah from entering Paradise, and the abode of such a person would be Hell.

ASPECT 1

THE DIVIDING LINE BETWEEN FAITH AND DISBELIEF

وَهَذِهِ هِيَ الْـمَسْأَلَةُ الَّتِـي تَفَرَّقَ النَّاسُ لِأَجْلِهَا بَيْــنَ مُسْلِمٍ وَكَافِرٍ، وَعِنْدَهَا وَقَعَتِ الْعَدَاوَةُ، وَلِأَجْلِهَا شُرِعَ الْـجِهَادُ، كَمَا قَالَ تَعَالَى: ﴿ وَقَٰتِلُوهُمْ حَتَّىٰ لَا تَكُونَ فِتْنَةٌ وَيَكُونَ ٱلدِّينُ كُلُّهُۥ لِلَّهِ ﴾ [الأنفال: ٣٩].

This is the issue that caused Mankind to split into Muslims and disbelievers. Over it, religious animosity occurs, and jihad (military confrontation) was legislated, as He, the Most High, says: "And fight them until there remains no fitnah (polytheism) and the Religion is entirely for Allah." [8:39]

الثَّانِيَةُ: أَنَّهُمْ مُتَفَرِّقُونَ فِي دِينِهِمْ، كَمَا قَالَ تَعَالَى: ﴿ كُلُّ حِزْبٍ بِمَا لَدَيْهِمْ فَرِحُونَ ﴾ [الروم: ٣٢]، وَكَذَلِكَ فِي دُنْيَاهُمْ، وَيَرَوْنَ أَنَّ ذَلِكَ هُوَ الصَّوَابُ، فَأَتَى بِالِاجْتِمَاعِ فِي الدِّينِ بِقَوْلِهِ: ﴿ شَرَعَ لَكُم مِّنَ ٱلدِّينِ مَا وَصَّىٰ بِهِۦ نُوحًا وَٱلَّذِىٓ أَوْحَيْنَآ إِلَيْكَ وَمَا وَصَّيْنَا بِهِۦٓ إِبْرَٰهِيمَ وَمُوسَىٰ وَعِيسَىٰٓ أَنْ أَقِيمُوا۟ ٱلدِّينَ وَلَا تَتَفَرَّقُوا۟ فِيهِ ﴾ [الشورى: ١٣].

THE SECOND ASPECT: *They were divided in their religion, as He, the Most High, says: "Each party would rejoice with what it had." [30:32] Likewise, in their worldly matters [they were also divided]. They considered this [division] to be correct. In contrast, He (Allah) sent them [orders of] religious solidarity, saying: "He has legislated for you in the Religion what He enjoined upon Nooh (Noah), that which He sent as revelation to you, and that which He enjoined upon Ibraaheem (Abraham), Moosaa (Moses), and 'Eesaa (Jesus): That you establish the Religion and do not be divided within it." [42:13]*

ASPECT 2

SPLITTING INTO RELIGIOUS FACTIONS (CONT'D)

وَقَالَ تَعَـالَـى: ﴿ إِنَّ ٱلَّذِينَ فَرَّقُواْ دِينَهُمْ وَكَانُواْ شِيَعًا لَّسْتَ مِنْهُمْ فِي شَيْءٍ ﴾ [الأنعام: ١٥٩]. وَنَهَانَا عَنْ مُشَابَهَتِهِمْ بِقَوْلِهِ: ﴿ وَلَا تَكُونُواْ كَٱلَّذِينَ تَفَرَّقُواْ وَٱخْتَلَفُواْ مِنْ بَعْدِ مَا جَاءَهُمُ ٱلْبَيِّنَٰتُ ﴾ [آل عمران: ١٠٥]، وَنَـهَانَا عَنِ التَّفَرُّقِ فِـي الدِّيْنِ بِقَوْلِهِ: ﴿ وَٱعْتَصِمُواْ بِحَبْلِ ٱللَّهِ جَمِيعًا وَلَا تَفَرَّقُواْ ﴾ [آل عمران: ١٠٣].

Also, He, the Most High, says: "Verily, those who split up their religion and became sects, you have nothing at all to do with them." [7:159] He has even forbidden us from resembling them, with His Statement: "Do not be like those who split up and differed after clear evidences came to them." [3:105] Additionally, He has forbidden us from splitting into religious sects with His Statement: "Hold fast to the Rope of Allah, all together, and do not be divided." [3:103]

ASPECT 3

DISREGARDING AND OPPOSING THE AUTHORITIES

الثَّالِثَةُ: أَنَّ مُخَالَفَةَ وَلِيِّ الْأَمْرِ وَعَدَمَ الِانْقِيَادِ لَهُ فَضِيلَةٌ، وَالسَّمْعَ وَالطَّاعَةَ لَهُ ذُلٌّ وَمَهَانَةٌ، فَخَالَفَهُمْ رَسُولُ اللهِ صَلَّى اللهُ عَلَيْهِ وَسَلَّمَ، وَأَمَرَ بِالصَّبْرِ عَلَى جَوْرِ الْوُلَاةِ، وَأَمَرَ بِالسَّمْعِ وَالطَّاعَةِ لَهُمْ وَالنَّصِيحَةِ، وَغَلَّظَ فِي ذَلِكَ، وَأَبْدَى فِيهِ وَأَعَادَ.

THE THIRD ASPECT: They considered opposing the leader and not recognizing his authority to be virtuous, while hearing and obeying was considered lowly and disgraceful. So, the Messenger of Allah, may Allah raise his rank and grant him peace, opposed them and ordered [the people] to be patient with the leaders' transgressions. He ordered them to hear, obey, and offer advice. He emphasized this greatly, time and time again.

ASPECTS 1-3

THE SIGNIFICANCE OF THESE FIRST THREE ASPECTS

وَهذِهِ الْمَسَائِلُ الثَّلَاثُ هِيَ الَّتِي جَمَعَ بَيْنَهَا فِيمَا صَحَّ عَنْهُ صَلَّى اللهُ عَلَيْهِ وَسَلَّمَ فِي الصَّحِيْحَيْنِ أَنَّهُ قَالَ: «إِنَّ اللهَ يَرْضَى لَكُمْ ثَلَاثًا: أَنْ تَعْبُدُوهُ، وَلَا تُشْرِكُوا بِهِ شَيْئًا، وَأَنْ تَعْتَصِمُوا بِحَبْلِ اللهِ جَمِيعًا وَلَا تَفَرَّقُوا، وَأَنْ تُنَاصِحُوا مَنْ وَلَّاهُ اللهُ أَمْرَكُمْ»، وَلَـــمْ يَقَعْ خَلَلٌ فِـــي دِينِ النَّاسِ وَدُنْيَاهُمْ إِلَّا بِسَبَبِ الْإِخْلَالِ فِـــي هَذِهِ الثَّلَاثِ أَوْ بَعْضِهَا.

These three issues have been mentioned all together in what was authentically recorded from him, may Allah raise his rank and grant him peace, in the two Saheeh compilations, that he said: "Verily, Allah is pleased with three things for you: That you worship Him without ascribing any partners to Him at all, that you hold fast to the Rope of Allah, all together, without being divided, and that you advise those whom Allah has placed in charge of your affair." There has never been any deficiency in the people's Religious or worldly affairs, except that it was due to a lapse in these three matters, or in some of them.

ASPECT 4

الرَّابِعَةُ: أَنَّ دِينَهُمْ مَبْنِيٌّ عَلَى أُصُولٍ أَعْظَمُهَا التَّقْلِيدُ، فَهُوَ الْقَاعِدَةُ الْكُبْرَى لِجَمِيعِ الْكُفَّارِ أَوَّلِهِمْ وَآخِرِهِمْ، كَمَا قَالَ تَعَالَى: ﴿ وَكَذَلِكَ مَا أَرْسَلْنَا مِن قَبْلِكَ فِي قَرْيَةٍ مِّن نَّذِيرٍ إِلَّا قَالَ مُتْرَفُوهَا إِنَّا وَجَدْنَا ءَابَاءَنَا عَلَىٰ أُمَّةٍ وَإِنَّا عَلَىٰ ءَاثَرِهِم مُّقْتَدُونَ ﴾ [الزخرف: ٢٣]، وَقَالَ تَعَالَى: ﴿ وَإِذَا قِيلَ لَهُمُ اتَّبِعُوا مَا أَنزَلَ اللَّهُ قَالُوا بَلْ نَتَّبِعُ مَا وَجَدْنَا عَلَيْهِ ءَابَاءَنَا أَوَلَوْ كَانَ الشَّيْطَانُ يَدْعُوهُمْ إِلَىٰ عَذَابِ السَّعِيرِ ﴾ [لقمان: ٢١].

THE FOURTH ASPECT: Their religion was based on certain foundations, the greatest of which was blind following. This has always been the core principle of all disbelievers, the first and last of them, as He, the Most High, says: "And thus We sent no warner before you to any nation, except that their extravagant ones said: We found our forefathers upon a way, so we shall remain following in their footsteps." [43:23] He, the Exalted, also says: "When it is said to them: Follow what Allah has revealed! They say: Instead, we shall follow what we found our fathers upon! Even if the Shaytaan were calling them to the torment of the Blazing Fire?!" [31:21]

فَأَتَاهُمْ بِقَوْلِهِ: ﴿ قُلْ إِنَّمَآ أَعِظُكُم بِوَٰحِدَةٍ أَن تَقُومُواْ لِلَّهِ مَثْنَىٰ وَفُرَٰدَىٰ ثُمَّ تَتَفَكَّرُواْ مَا بِصَاحِبِكُم مِّن جِنَّةٍ ﴾، الآيَةَ [سبأ: ٤٦]، وَقَوْلِهِ: ﴿ ٱتَّبِعُواْ مَآ أُنزِلَ إِلَيْكُم مِّن رَّبِّكُمْ وَلَا تَتَّبِعُواْ مِن دُونِهِۦ أَوْلِيَآءَ قَلِيلًا مَّا تَذَكَّرُونَ ﴾ [الأعراف: ٣].

So He delivered His Word to them: "Say: I only admonish you with a single thing – that you stand up [in worship] unto Allah [alone], in groups and individually, and then reflect. There is no demon possessing your companion!" [34:46] And He says: "Follow that which has come down to you from your Lord, and do not follow others less than Him, [taking them] as protectors. Little is the reflection you offer." [7:3]

ASPECT 5

THE MAJORITY VOTE: BEING DELUDED BY NUMBERS

الـخَامِسَةُ: أَنَّ مِنْ أَكْبَرِ قَوَاعِدِهِمُ الإغْتِـرَارَ بِالأَكْثَرِ، وَيَـحْتَجُّونَ بِهِ عَلَى صِحَّةِ الشَّـيْءِ، وَيَسْـتَدِلُّونَ عَلَى بُطْلَانِ الشَّـيْءِ بِغُرْبَتِهِ، وَقِلَّةِ أَهْلِهِ، فَأَتَاهُمْ بِضِـدِّ ذَلِكَ، وَأَوْضَحَهُ فِي غَيْرِ مَوْضِعٍ مِنَ القُرْآنِ.

THE FIFTH ASPECT: From their most central foundations was to be influenced by the majority. They would cite the majority as their evidence for something's correctness. Thus, their proof for something being false would be [merely] its strangeness and the limited number of its supporters. So, He sent them [Revelation proving] the opposite of that and clarified it in more than one passage of the Quran.

ASPECT 6

USING THE WAYS OF THE ANCESTORS AS PROOFS

السَّادِسَةُ: الاِحْتِجَاجُ بِالـمُتَقَدِّمِينَ، كَقَوْلِهِ: ﴿ قَالَ فَمَا بَالُ ٱلْقُرُونِ ٱلْأُولَىٰ ﴾ [طه: ٥١]، ﴿ مَّا سَمِعْنَا بِهَـٰذَا فِىٓ ءَابَآئِنَا ٱلْأَوَّلِينَ ﴾ [المؤمنين: ٢٤].

THE SIXTH ASPECT: Using ancestors as proofs, like [what is found] in His Statement: "So then what about the first generations?!" [20:51] Also, "We have not heard of this from our forefathers of old!" [23:24]

ASPECT 7

USING THE RICH AND POWERFUL AS PROOFS

السَّابِعَةُ: الاسْتِدْلَالُ بِقَوْمٍ أُعْطُواْ قُوَى فِي الأَفْهَامِ وَالأَعْمَالِ، وَفِي المُلْكِ وَالمَالِ وَالجَاهِ، فَرَدَّ اللهُ ذَلِكَ بِقَوْلِهِ: ﴿ وَلَقَدْ مَكَّنَّهُمْ فِيمَا إِن مَّكَّنَّكُمْ فِيهِ ﴾ [الأحقاف: ٢٦]، وَقَوْلِهِ: ﴿ وَكَانُواْ مِن قَبْلُ يَسْتَفْتِحُونَ عَلَى ٱلَّذِينَ كَفَرُواْ فَلَمَّا جَاءَهُم مَّا عَرَفُواْ كَفَرُواْ بِهِۦ ﴾ [البقرة: ٨٩]، وَقَوْلِهِ: ﴿ يَعْرِفُونَهُۥ كَمَا يَعْرِفُونَ أَبْنَاءَهُمْ ﴾ [البقرة: ١٤٦].

THE SEVENTH ASPECT: Citing [the behavior of] those given strength in understanding, deeds, authority, wealth, and/or status as evidence. Allah responded to that with His Statement: "And We certainly did enable them in ways We have not enabled you in." [46:26]
And His Statement: "They had previously sought victory over those who has disbelieved, yet when there came to them what they were familiar with, they disbelieved in it." [2:89]
And His Statement: "They know him as much as they know their own children." [2:146]

ASPECT 8

REJECTING THE TRUTH BECAUSE THE WEAK FOLLOW IT

الثَّامِنَةُ: الاِسْتِدْلَالُ عَلَى بُطْلَانِ الشَّيْءِ بِأَنَّهُ لَــمْ يَتَّبِعْهُ إِلَّا الضُّعَفَاءُ، كَقَوْلِهِ: ﴿ قَالُوٓاْ أَنُؤْمِنُ لَكَ وَاتَّبَعَكَ الْأَرْذَلُونَ ﴾ [الشــعراء: ١١١]، وَقَوْلِهِ: ﴿ أَهَٰٓؤُلَآءِ مَنَّ اللَّهُ عَلَيْهِم مِّنْ بَيْنِنَآ ﴾، فَرَدَّهُ اللهُ بِقَوْلِهِ: ﴿ أَلَيْسَ اللَّهُ بِأَعْلَمَ بِالشَّـٰكِرِينَ ﴾ [الأنعام: ٥٣].

THE EIGHTH ASPECT: Trying to disprove something by claiming only the weak and meager follow it, like [what is found in] His Statement: "Shall we believe for you whilst the most meagre [of the people] follow you?!" [26:111] And His Statement: "Are such [poor] people favored by Allah from among us?" To which He responded with His Statement: "Is not Allah most knowledgeable about those who are truly grateful?" [6:53]

ASPECT 9

TAKING EVIL SCHOLARS AS ROLE MODELS

التَّاسِعَةُ: الاقْتِدَاءُ بِفَسَقَةِ العُلَمَاءِ، فَأَتَى بِقَوْلِهِ: ﴿ يَـٰٓأَيُّهَا ٱلَّذِينَ ءَامَنُوٓاْ إِنَّ كَثِيرًا مِّنَ ٱلْأَحْبَارِ وَٱلرُّهْبَانِ لَيَأْكُلُونَ أَمْوَٰلَ ٱلنَّاسِ بِٱلْبَٰطِلِ وَيَصُدُّونَ عَن سَبِيلِ ٱللَّهِ ﴾ [التوبة: ٣٤]، وَقَوْلِهِ: ﴿ لَا تَغْلُواْ فِى دِينِكُمْ غَيْرَ ٱلْحَقِّ وَلَا تَتَّبِعُوٓاْ أَهْوَآءَ قَوْمٍ قَدْ ضَلُّواْ مِن قَبْلُ وَأَضَلُّواْ كَثِيرًا وَضَلُّواْ عَن سَوَآءِ ٱلسَّبِيلِ ﴾ [المائدة: ٧٧].

THE NINTH ASPECT: Taking evil scholars as role models, and so He sent them His Statement: "O you who have believed! Indeed, there are many priests and monks who devour the people's wealth in falsehood, while they block [them] from the path of Allah." [9:34] And His Statement: "Do not go to extremes in your religion, but just [follow] the Truth. And do not follow the desires of a people who have gone astray long ago, those who misguided many, straying themselves far from the correct path." [5:77]

ASPECT 10

CLAIMS ABOUT THE FOLLOWERS OF THE TRUTH

العَاشِرَةُ: الاِسْتِدْلَالُ عَلَى بُطْلَانِ الدِّيْنِ بِقِلَّةِ أَفْهَامِ أَهْلِهِ، وَعَدَمِ حِفْظِهِمْ، كَقَوْلِهِمْ: ﴿ بَادِيَ ٱلرَّأْيِ ﴾ [هود: ٢٧].

THE TENTH ASPECT: Claiming that the falsity of a religion is proven by the poor understanding of some of its adherents, and their lack of memorization, like their statement [referring to the followers of the Prophets]: "Those of simple, undeveloped (primitive) opinions." [11:27]

ASPECT 11

USING FALSE ANALOGIES AS PROOFS

الـحَادِيَةَ عَشْرَةَ: الاِسْتِدْلَالُ بِالقِيَاسِ الفَاسِدِ، كَقَوْلِـهِمْ:

﴿ إِنْ أَنتُمْ إِلَّا بَشَرٌ مِّثْلُنَا ﴾ [إبراهيم: ١٠].

THE ELEVENTH ASPECT: Using false analogies as proofs, like their statement: "You are only human beings like us." [14:10]

ASPECT 12

REJECTING SOUND ANALOGIES

الثَّانِيَةَ عَشْرَةَ: إِنْكَارُ القِيَاسِ الصَّحِيْحِ، وَالــجَامِعُ لِــهَذَا وَمَا قَبْلَهُ عَدَمُ فَهْمِ الجَامِعِ وَالفَارِقِ.

THE TWELFTH ASPECT: Rejecting sound analogies. This aspect and the previous one share something in common. They both result from not understanding why issues are similar and should share the same ruling, and why other issues are different and deserve different rulings.

ASPECT 13

FANATICISM TOWARDS THE SCHOLARS & RIGHTEOUS

الثَّالِثَةَ عَشْرَةَ: الغُلُوُّ فِي العُلَمَاءِ وَالصَّالِحِينَ، كَقَوْلِهِ: ﴿يَٰٓأَهْلَ ٱلْكِتَٰبِ لَا تَغْلُوا۟ فِى دِينِكُمْ وَلَا تَقُولُوا۟ عَلَى ٱللَّهِ إِلَّا ٱلْحَقَّ﴾ [النساء: ١٧١].

THE THIRTEENTH ASPECT: Having fanaticism towards the scholars and the righteous people, like His Statement: "O People of the Book! Do not go to excesses in your religion! And do not say regarding Allah except the Truth." [4:171]

ASPECT 14

MISGUIDED NEGATIONS & AFFIRMATIONS

الرَّابِعَةَ عَشْـــرَةَ: أَنَّ كُلَّ مَا تَقَدَّمَ مَبْنِـــيٌّ عَلَى قَاعِدَةٍ وَهِيَ النَّفْيُ وَالإِثْبَاتُ، فَيَتَّبِعُونَ الْهَوَى وَالظَّنَّ، وَيُعْرِضُونَ عَمَّا جَاءَتْ بِهِ الرُّسُلُ.

THE FOURTEENTH ASPECT, which is the underlying principle behind everything which has preceded: Negating [what Allah has affirmed] and affirming [what He has negated]. They merely follow desires and conjecture, while they turn away from what the Messengers came with.

ASPECT 15

PRETENDING NOT TO UNDERSTAND THE TRUTH

الْخَامِسَةَ عَشْرَةَ: اعْتِذَارُهُمْ عَنِ اتِّبَاعِ مَا آتَاهُمُ اللهُ بِعَدَمِ الْفَهْمِ، كَقَوْلِهِ: ﴿ وَقَالُوا

قُلُوبُنَا غُلْفٌ ﴾ [البقرة: ٨٨]، ﴿ يَاشُعَيْبُ مَا نَفْقَهُ كَثِيرًا مِّمَّا تَقُولُ ﴾ [هود: ٩١]،

فَأَكْذَبَهُمُ اللهُ، وَبَيَّنَ أَنَّ ذَلِكَ بِسَبَبِ الطَّبْعِ عَلَى قُلُوبِهِمْ، وَأَنَّ الطَّبْعَ بِسَبَبِ كُفْرِهِمْ.

THE FIFTEENTH ASPECT: Excusing themselves from following what Allah had given them, claiming that they do not understand it, like His Statement: "They said: Our hearts are incapable of understanding." [2:88] And: "O Shu'ayb! We do not understand much of what you are saying!" [11:91] So Allah exposed them as liars and clarified that it was because of a seal upon their hearts, a seal that was the result of their own disbelief.

ASPECT 16

TRADING IN REVELATION FOR BOOKS OF MAGIC

السَّادِسَةَ عَشْرَةَ: اعْتِيَاضُهُمْ عَمَّا أَتَاهُمْ مِنَ اللهِ بِكُتُبِ السِّحْرِ، كَمَا ذَكَرَ اللهُ ذَلِكَ فِي قَوْلِهِ: ﴿ نَبَذَ فَرِيقٌ مِّنَ ٱلَّذِينَ أُوتُواْ ٱلْكِتَٰبَ كِتَٰبَ ٱللَّهِ وَرَآءَ ظُهُورِهِمْ كَأَنَّهُمْ لَا يَعْلَمُونَ ۝ وَٱتَّبَعُواْ مَا تَتْلُواْ ٱلشَّيَٰطِينُ عَلَىٰ مُلْكِ سُلَيْمَٰنَ﴾ [البقرة: ١٠١–١٠٢].

THE SIXTEENTH ASPECT: Replacing what had come to them from Allah with books of magic. Allah mentions this in His Statement: "A group of those given Scripture cast the Book of Allah behind their backs, as if they had no knowledge. Instead, they followed that [magic] which the devils recited during the reign of Sulaymaan (Solomon)." [2:101-102]

ASPECT 17

ATTRIBUTING THEIR OWN FALSEHOOD TO THE PROPHETS

السَّابِعَةَ عَشْرَةَ: نِسْبَةُ بَاطِلِهِمْ إِلَـــى الأَنْبِيَاءِ، كَقَوْلِهِ: ﴿ وَمَا كَفَرَ سُلَيْمَنُ ﴾ [البقرة: ١٠٢]، وَقَوْلِهِ: ﴿ مَا كَانَ إِبْرَهِيمُ يَهُودِيًّا وَلَا نَصْرَانِيًّا ﴾ [آل عمران: ٦٧].

THE SEVENTEENTH ASPECT: Attributing their own falsehood to the Prophets, like [what is referred to in] His Statement: "Yet Sulaymaan (Solomon) did not disbelieve," [2:102] and His Statement: "Ibraaheem (Abraham) was not a Jew, nor was he a Christian." [3:67]

ASPECT 18

FALSE & CONTRADICTORY ASCRIPTIONS

الثَّامِنَةَ عَشْرَةَ: تَنَاقُضُهُمْ فِــي الِانْتِسَابِ، يَنْتَسِبُونَ إِلَــى إِبْرَاهِيمَ، مَعَ إِظْهَارِهِمْ تَرْكَ اتِّبَاعِهِ.

THE EIGHTEENTH ASPECT: *Contradictory ascriptions, as they would ascribe to Ibraaheem (Abraham), along with their blatant lack of following him.*

ASPECT 19

REVILING THE RIGHTEOUS BECAUSE OF THEIR FOLLOWERS

التَّاسِعَةَ عَشْرَةَ: قَدْحُهُمْ فِي بَعْضِ الصَّالِحِيْنَ بِفِعْلِ بَعْضِ الْمُنْتَسِبِيْنَ إِلَيْهِمْ، كَقَدْحِ الْيَهُودِ فِي عِيسَى، وَقَدْحِ الْيَهُودِ وَالنَّصَارَى فِي مُحَمَّدٍ صَلَّى اللهُ عَلَيْهِ وَسَلَّمَ.

THE NINETEENTH ASPECT: Reviling righteous people based on the actions of some of those who ascribed to them, like how the Jews reviled 'Eesaa (Jesus), and how both the Jews and Christians reviled Muhammad, may Allah raise his rank and grant him peace.

Knowledge comes from ongoing effort, and level by level, whoever diligently seeks knowledge will be granted it.

ASPECT 20

CONSIDERING MAGIC TRICKS A SIGN OF PIETY

العِشْرُونَ: اعْتِقَادُهُمْ فِي مَـخَارِيقِ السَّحَرَةِ وَأَمْثَالِــهِمْ أَنَّــهَا مِنْ كَرَامَاتِ الصَّالِحِينَ، وَنِسْبَتُهُ إِلَى الأَنْبِيَاءِ، كَمَا نَسَبُوهُ لِسُلَيْمَانَ عَلَيْهِ السَّلَامُ.

THE TWENTIETH ASPECT: *Their belief that tricks of magicians and similar charlatans were miraculous signs of righteousness, attributing that [idea] to the Prophets, like how they attributed it to Sulaymaan (Solomon), may Allah grant him peace.*

ASPECTS 21-22

WHISTLING, CLAPPING, & FRIVOLITY AS WORSHIP

الْحَادِيَةُ وَالْعِشْرُونَ: تَعَبُّدُهُمْ بِالْمُكَاءِ وَالتَّصْدِيَةِ.

THE TWENTY-FIRST ASPECT: They would whistle and clap as worship.

الثَّانِيَةُ وَالْعِشْرُونَ: أَنَّهُمُ اتَّخَذُوا دِينَهُمْ لَهْوًا وَلَعِبًا.

THE TWENTY-SECOND ASPECT: They took their religion as frivolity and amusement.

ASPECT 23

BEING DELUDED BY THEIR WORLDLY PROSPERITY

الثَّالِثَةُ وَالعِشْرُونَ: أَنَّ الحَيَاةَ الدُّنْيَا غَرَّتْهُمْ، فَظَنُّوا أَنَّ عَطَاءَ اللهِ مِنْهَا يَدُلُّ عَلَى رِضَاهُ، كَقَوْلِهِمْ: ﴿ نَحْنُ أَكْثَرُ أَمْوَالًا وَأَوْلَادًا وَمَا نَحْنُ بِمُعَذَّبِينَ ﴾ [سبأ: ٣٥].

THE TWENTY-THIRD ASPECT: They were deluded by this worldly life, as they presumed that [receiving] Allah's provisions was proof of His approval [of them and their actions], like their statement: "We have more wealth and children, and we are not going to be punished." [34:35]

ASPECT 24

REJECTING TRUTH BECAUSE THE WEAK EMBRACED IT FIRST

الرَّابِعَةُ وَالعِشْرُونَ: تَرْكُ الدُّخُولِ فِي الـحَقِّ إِذَا سَبَقَهُمْ إِلَيْهِ الضُّعَفَاءُ تَكَبُّرًا وَأَنَفَةً،

فَأَنْزَلَ اللهُ تَعَالَى: ﴿ وَلَا تَطْرُدِ ٱلَّذِينَ يَدْعُونَ رَبَّهُم ﴾، الآيَاتِ [الأنعام: ٥٢].

THE TWENTY-FOURTH ASPECT: Refusal to embrace the Truth because the weak and meager had already preceded them to it, out of arrogance and disdain. Allah, the Most High, sent down: "Do not dismiss those who call upon their Lord..." [6:52]

ASPECT 25

Taking the Previous Aspect a Step Further

الـخَامِسَةُ وَالعِشْرُونَ: الِاسْتِدْلَالُ عَلَى بُطْلَانِهِ بِسَبْقِ الضُّعَفَاءِ كَقَوْلِهِ:

﴿ لَوْ كَانَ خَيْرًا مَّا سَبَقُونَا إِلَيْهِ ﴾ [الأحقاف: ١١].

THE TWENTY-FIFTH ASPECT: Citing as a proof of something's falsehood that the weak and meager preceded them to it, like [what is found in] His Statement: "Had it been something good, they would not have preceded us to it." [46:11]

ASPECT 26

CHANGING THE BOOK OF ALLAH INTENTIONALLY

السَّادِسَةُ وَالعِشْرُونَ: تَحْرِيفُ كِتَابِ اللهِ مِنْ بَعْدِ مَا عَقَلُوهُ وَهُمْ يَعْلَمُونَ.

THE TWENTY-SIXTH ASPECT: Changing the Book of Allah, after having understood it, whilst they had knowledge.

ASPECT 27

INVENTING FALSE SCRIPTURE & ATTRIBUTING IT TO ALLAH

السَّابِعَةُ وَالعِشْرُونَ: تَصْنِيفُ الكُتُبِ البَاطِلَةِ وَنِسْبَتُهَا إِلَـــى اللهِ، كَقَوْلِهِ: ﴿ فَوَيْلٌ لِّلَّذِينَ يَكْتُبُونَ ٱلْكِتَبَ بِأَيْدِيهِمْ ثُمَّ يَقُولُونَ هَذَا مِنْ عِندِ ٱللَّهِ ﴾ [البقرة: ٧٩].

THE TWENTY-SEVENTH ASPECT: Concocting false scripture and attributing it to Allah, like His Statement: "Woe to those who write the book with their own hands and then say: This is from Allah." [2:79]

ASPECT 28

NOT ACCEPTING TRUTH FROM OUTSIDE THEIR GROUP

الثَّامِنَةُ وَالعِشْرُونَ: أَنَّـهُمْ لَا يَقْبَلُونَ مِنَ الـحَقِّ إِلَّا الَّذِي مَعَ طَائِفَتِهِمْ، كَقَوْلِهِ: ﴿ قَالُواْ نُؤْمِنُ بِمَآ أُنزِلَ عَلَيْنَا ﴾ [البقرة: ٩١].

THE TWENTY-EIGHTH ASPECT: *Refusal to accept anything of the Truth which it is not found with their group, like His Statement: "They said: We only believe in what was sent down to us." [2:91]*

ASPECT 29

NOT EVEN TRULY PRACTICING THEIR OWN RELIGION

التَّاسِعَةُ وَالعِشْرُونَ: أَنَّهُمْ مَعَ ذَلِكَ لَا يَعْمَلُونَ بِمَا تَقُولُهُ طَائِفَتُهُمْ كَمَا نَبَّهَ اللهُ تَعَالَى عَلَيْهِ بِقَوْلِهِ: ﴿ قُلْ فَلِمَ تَقْتُلُونَ أَنْبِيَاءَ اللَّهِ مِن قَبْلُ إِن كُنتُم مُّؤْمِنِينَ ﴾ [البقرة: ٩١].

THE TWENTY-NINTH ASPECT: Even with that [the previous aspect], they would not really act upon what their group believed anyway, as Allah, the Most High, noted in His Statement: "Say: Why then have you killed the Prophets of Allah before, if you are indeed believers?" [2:91]

ASPECT 30

EACH GROUP REJOICING WITH WHAT THEY HAVE

الثَّلَاثُونَ: وَهِيَ مِنْ عَجَائِبِ آيَاتِ اللهِ أَنَّهُمْ لَمَّا تَرَكُوا وَصِيَّةَ اللهِ بِالِاجْتِمَاعِ، وَارْتَكَبُوا مَا نَهَى اللهُ عَنْهُ مِنَ الِافْتِرَاقِ، صَارَ كُلُّ حِزْبٍ بِمَا لَدَيْهِمْ فَرِحِينَ.

THE THIRTIETH ASPECT, which is from the amazing signs of Allah: After abandoning Allah's Order for unity, they would fall into the differing that Allah forbade them from, each group rejoicing with what they had.

ASPECT 31

HYPOCRITICAL HATRED FOR WHAT THEY ASCRIBED TO

الــحَادِيَةُ وَالثَّلَاثُونَ: وَهِيَ مِنْ أَعْجَبِ الآيَاتِ أَيْضًا، مُعَادَاتُـهُمْ الدِّيْنَ الَّذِي انْتَسَبُوا إِلَيْهِ غَايَةَ العَدَاوَةِ، وَمَـحَبَّتُهُمْ دِيْنَ الكُفَّارِ الَّذِينَ عَادَوْهُمْ وَعَادَوْا نَبِيَّهُمْ وَفِئَتَهُمْ غَايَةَ الـمَحَبَّةِ، كَمَا فَعَلُوا مَعَ النَّبِيِّ صَلَّى اللهُ عَلَيْهِ وَسَلَّمَ لَـمَّا أَتَاهُمْ بِدِيْنِ مُوسَى عَلَيْهِ السَّلَامُ، وَاتَّبَعُوا كُتُبَ السِّحْرِ، وَهِيَ مِنْ دِيْنِ آلِ فِرْعَوْنَ.

THE THIRTY-FIRST ASPECT, which is also from the most amazing of signs: Their unmatched animosity for the very religion they ascribed to, along with their love of the religion of the disbelievers who despise them and their Prophet. They would love such people with unparalleled love, as they did when the Prophet, may Allah raise his rank and grant him peace, came to them with the Religion of Moosaa (Moses), peace be upon him. They preferred to follow books of magic instead, which was actually from the religion of Pharaoh's people!

ASPECT 32

DESPISING PEOPLE, REJECTING THE TRUTH THEY HAVE

الثَّانِيَةُ وَالثَّلَاثُونَ: كُفْرُهُمْ بِالْحَقِّ إِذَا كَانَ مَعَ مَنْ لَا يَهْوَونَهُ، كَمَا قَالَ تَعَالَى:

﴿ وَقَالَتِ ٱلْيَهُودُ لَيْسَتِ ٱلنَّصَرَىٰ عَلَىٰ شَيْءٍ وَقَالَتِ ٱلنَّصَرَىٰ لَيْسَتِ ٱلْيَهُودُ عَلَىٰ شَيْءٍ ﴾

[البقرة: ١١٣].

THE THIRTY-SECOND ASPECT: Their disbelief in the Truth when it was found with those they did not admire, as Allah, the Most High, says: "The Jews said that the Christians were not upon anything, while the Christians said that the Jews were not upon anything." [2:113]

ASPECT 33

REJECTING PARTS OF THEIR OWN RELIGION

الثَّالِثَةُ وَالثَّلَاثُونَ: إِنْكَارُهُمْ مَا أَقَرُّوا أَنَّهُ مِنْ دِينِهِمْ، كَمَا فَعَلُوا فِي حَجِّ الْبَيْتِ،

فَقَالَ تَعَالَى: ﴿ وَمَن يَرْغَبُ عَن مِّلَّةِ إِبْرَاهِيمَ إِلَّا مَن سَفِهَ نَفْسَهُ ﴾ [البقرة: ١٣٠].

THE THIRTY-THIRD ASPECT: *Rejecting what they had previously acknowledged to be part of their own religion, like what they did regarding Hajj to the House, as Allah, the Most High, says: "Who would be inclined against the Religion of Ibraaheem (Abraham) other than one who makes a fool of himself?" [2:130]*

ASPECT 34

EVERY SECT CLAIMED IT WAS THE SAVED ONE

الرَّابِعَةُ وَالثَّلَاثُونَ: أَنَّ كُلَّ فِرْقَةٍ تَدَّعِي أَنَّــهَا النَّاجِيَةُ، فَأَكْذَبَــــهُمُ اللهُ بِقَوْلِهِ:

﴿ هَاتُواْ بُرْهَانَكُمْ إِن كُنتُمْ صَادِقِينَ ﴾ [البقرة: ١١١]، ثُمَّ بَيَّـنَ الصَّوَابَ

بِقَوْلِهِ: ﴿ بَلَى مَنْ أَسْلَمَ وَجْهَهُ لِلَّهِ وَهُوَ مُحْسِنٌ ﴾ [البقرة: ١١٢].

THE THIRTY-FOURTH ASPECT: Every religious sect would claim that it was the saved one, so Allah exposed them as liars with His Statement: "Bring forth your proof if you are indeed truthful." [2:111] Then, He clarified the correct way with His Statement: "Nay! He who submits his face unto Allah, being a person of sincere worship…" [2:112]

ASPECT 35

NAKEDNESS AS A FORM OF WORSHIP

الــخَامِسَةُ وَالثَّلَاثُونَ: التَّعَبُّدُ بِكَشْفِ العَوْرَاتِ، كَقَوْلِهِ: ﴿ وَإِذَا فَعَلُوا فَاحِشَةً قَالُوا وَجَدْنَا عَلَيْهَا ءَابَاءَنَا وَٱللَّهُ أَمَرَنَا بِهَا ﴾ [الأعراف: ٢٨].

THE THIRTY-FIFTH ASPECT: Worshipping with uncovered private parts, as found in His Statement: "When they would commit an obscenity, they would say: We found our fathers doing this, and Allah has ordered us to do it." [7:28]

ASPECT 36

FORBIDDING PERMISSIBLE THINGS AS PIETY

السَّادِسَةُ وَالثَّلَاثُونَ: التَّعَبُّدُ بِتَحْرِيمِ الحَلَالِ، كَمَا تَعَبَّدُوا بِالشِّرْكِ.

THE THIRTY-SIXTH ASPECT: Forbidding permissible things as an act of religiosity, whilst also engaging in [forbidden] polytheistic worship.

ASPECT 37

TAKING PRIESTS & MONKS AS LORDS BESIDE ALLAH

السَّابِعَةُ وَالثَّلَاثُونَ: التَّعَبُّدُ بِاتِّخَاذِ الْأَحْبَارِ وَالرُّهْبَانِ أَرْبَابًا مِنْ دُونِ اللهِ.

THE THIRTY-SEVENTH ASPECT: *Taking their priests and monks as lords beside Allah, as an act of religiosity.*

ASPECT 38

DEVIATION WITH REGARDS TO ALLAH'S ATTRIBUTES

الثَّامِنَةُ وَالثَّلَاثُونَ: الإِلْحَادُ فِي الصِّفَاتِ، كَقَوْلِهِ تَعَالَى: ﴿ وَ. . ظَنَنْتُمْ أَنَّ ٱللَّهَ لَا يَعْلَمُ كَثِيرًا مِّمَّا تَعْمَلُونَ ﴾ [فصلت: ٢٢].

THE THIRTY-EIGHTH ASPECT: Deviating with regards to the Divine Attributes [of Allah], as He, the Most High, says: "However, you presumed that Allah does not know much of what you do!" [41:22]

ASPECT 39

DEVIATION WITH REGARDS TO ALLAH'S NAMES

التَّاسِعَةُ وَالثَّلَاثُونَ: الْإِلْحَادُ فِي الْأَسْمَاءِ، كَقَوْلِهِ: ﴿وَهُمْ يَكْفُرُونَ بِالرَّحْمَنِ﴾ [الرعد: ٣٠].

THE THIRTY-NINTH ASPECT: Deviating with regards to the Names [of Allah], like His Statement: "And they disbelieve in ar-Rahmaan (the Most Gracious)." [13:30]

ASPECT 40

COMPLETE DENIAL OF ALLAH'S EXISTENCE

الأَرْبَعُونَ: التَّعْطِيلُ، كَقَوْلِ آلِ فِرْعَوْنَ.

THE FORTIETH ASPECT: Absolute denial [of the existence of Allah], similar to the belief of Pharaoh's people.

ASPECT 41

ATTRIBUTING DEFICIENCIES TO ALLAH

الــحَادِيَةُ وَالأَرْبَعُونَ: نِسْبَةُ النَّقَائِصِ إِلَيْهِ سُبْحَانَهُ، كَالوَلَدِ وَالحَاجَةِ وَالتَّعْبِ، مَعَ تَنْزِيهِ رُهْبَانِهِمْ عَنْ بَعْضِ ذَلِكَ.

THE FORTY-FIRST ASPECT: Attributing deficiencies to Him, the Exalted One, like having a child, being needy, and fatigue, while they would exalt their own religious leaders above some of those things!

ASPECT 42

ASCRIBING PARTNERS TO ALLAH IN HIS SOVEREIGNTY

الثَّانِيَةُ وَالأَرْبَعُونَ: الشِّرْكُ فِي المُلْكِ، كَقَوْلِ المَجُوسِ.

THE FORTY-SECOND ASPECT: Ascribing partners to Allah in His Dominion and Authority, like the belief of the Zoroastrians.

ASPECT 43

REJECTING QADAR (DIVINE DECREE)

الثَّالِثَةُ وَالأَرْبَعُونَ: جُحُودُ القَدَرِ.

THE FORTY-THIRD ASPECT: Rejecting Qadr (Divine Decree).

ASPECT 44

CONSIDERING QADAR A PROOF AGAINST ALLAH

الرَّابِعَةُ وَالأَرْبَعُونَ: الاِحْتِجَاجُ عَلَى اللهِ بِهِ.

THE FORTY-FOURTH ASPECT: Citing it (Qadr) as a proof
Against Allah [absolving themselves of accountability].

ASPECT 45

CONFUSION ABOUT THE QADAR OF ALLAH

الخَامِسَةُ وَالأَرْبَعُونَ: مُعَارَضَةُ شَرْعِ اللهِ بِقَدَرِهِ.

THE FORTY-FIFTH ASPECT: Claims of contradiction between Allah's Legislation and His Qadr (Divine Decree).

ASPECT 46
INAPPROPRIATE SPEECH ABOUT TIME

السَّادِسَةُ وَالأَرْبَعُونَ: مَسَبَّةُ الدَّهْرِ، كَقَوْلِهِمْ: ﴿ وَمَا يُهْلِكُنَآ إِلَّا ٱلدَّهْرُ ﴾ [الجاثية: ٢٤].

THE FORTY-SIXTH ASPECT: Speaking ill of time, like their statement: "Nothing causes us to perish other than [the passing of] time." [45:24]

ASPECT 47

CREDITING ALLAH'S BLESSINGS TO OTHERS

السَّابِعَةُ وَالأَرْبَعُونَ: إِضَافَةُ نِعَمِ اللهِ إِلَى غَيْرِهِ كَقَوْلِهِ: ﴿ يَعْرِفُونَ نِعْمَتَ اللَّهِ ثُمَّ يُنكِرُونَهَا ﴾ [النحل: ٨٣].

THE FORTY-SEVENTH ASPECT: *Ascribing Allah's blessings to others, like His Statement: "They recognize the blessing of Allah, yet they deny it." [16:83]*

ASPECTS 48-49

DISBELIEVING IN ALLAH'S VERSES

الثَّامِنَةُ وَالأَرْبَعُونَ: الكُفْرُ بِآيَاتِ اللهِ.

THE FORTY-EIGHTH ASPECT: *Disbelieving in the Verses of Allah.*

التَّاسِعَةُ وَالأَرْبَعُونَ: جَحْدُ بَعْضِهَا.

THE FORTY-NINTH ASPECT: *Rejecting some of them.*

ASPECT 50

CLAIMING REVELATION NEVER CAME TO A HUMAN BEING

الخَمْسُونَ: قَوْلُهُمْ: ﴿ مَآ أَنزَلَ ٱللَّهُ عَلَىٰ بَشَرٍ مِّن شَيْءٍ ﴾ [الأنعام: ٩١].

THE FIFTIETH ASPECT: Their statement: "Allah has not sent down to any human being any revelation at all." [6:91]

ASPECT 51

CLAIMING THE QURAN IS JUST HUMAN SPEECH

الْحَادِيَةُ وَالْخَمْسُونَ: قَوْلُهُمْ فِي الْقُرْآنِ: ﴿ إِنْ هَذَآ إِلَّا قَوْلُ ٱلْبَشَرِ ﴾ [المدثر: ٢٥].

THE FIFTY-FIRST ASPECT: Their statement about the Quran:
"This is nothing but the word of a human being." [74:25]

ASPECT 52

FINDING FAULT WITH ALLAH'S WISDOM

الثَّانِيَةُ وَالخَمْسُونَ: القَدْحُ فِي حِكْمَةِ اللهِ تَعَالَى.

THE FIFTY-SECOND ASPECT: Finding fault with the Wisdom of Allah, the Most High.

ASPECT 53

USING TRICKERY TO REPEL THE TRUTH

الثَّالِثَةُ وَالْـخَمْسُونَ: إِعْمَالُ الْـحِيَلِ الظَّاهِرَةِ وَالْبَاطِنَةِ فِي دَفْعِ مَا جَاءَتْ بِهِ الرُّسُلُ، كَقَوْلِهِ تَعَالَى: ﴿وَمَكَرُواْ وَمَكَرَ ٱللَّهُ﴾ [آل عمران: ٥٤]، وَقَوْلِهِ: ﴿وَقَالَت طَّآئِفَةٌ مِّنْ أَهْلِ ٱلْكِتَـٰبِ ءَامِنُواْ بِٱلَّذِىٓ أُنزِلَ عَلَى ٱلَّذِينَ ءَامَنُواْ وَجْهَ ٱلنَّهَارِ وَٱكْفُرُوٓاْ ءَاخِرَهُۥ﴾ [آل عمران: ٧٢].

THE FIFTY-THIRD ASPECT: Using both blatant and hidden trickery to repel what the Messengers have come with, like the Statement of the Most High: "And they plotted, while Allah plotted." [3:54] And His Statement: "A group of the People of the Book said: Believe in the morning in what has been sent down upon those who believe, then disbelieve at the end of the day." [3:72]

ASPECT 54

PRETENDING TO EMBRACE THE TRUTH AS A PLOT

الرَّابِعَةُ وَالخَمْسُونَ: الإِقْرَارُ بِالحَقِّ لِيَتَوَصَّلُوا بِهِ إِلَى دَفْعِهِ، كَمَا قَالَ فِي الآيَةِ.

THE FIFTY-FOURTH ASPECT: Pretending to acknowledge the Truth in order to plot against it, as He says in the Verse (3:72).

ASPECT 55
PARTISAN-BASED BIGOTRY FOR THEIR WAY

الخَامِسَةُ وَالخَمْسُونَ: التَّعَصُّبُ لِلْمَذْهَبِ، كَقَوْلِهِ تَعَالَى: ﴿ وَلَا تُؤْمِنُوٓاْ إِلَّا لِمَن تَبِعَ دِينَكُمۡ ﴾ [آل عمران: ٧٣].

THE FIFTY-FIFTH ASPECT: Partisan-based bigotry for their way, like the Statement of the Most High: "Do not believe except for one who follows your own religion." [3:73]

ASPECT 56

CALLING THE PRACTICE OF ISLAM "POLYTHEISM"

السَّادِسَةُ وَالـخَمْسُونَ: تَسْمِيَةُ اتِّبَاعِ الإِسْلَامِ شِرْكًا، كَمَا ذَكَرَهُ فِي قَوْلِهِ تَعَالَى: ﴿مَا كَانَ لِبَشَرٍ أَن يُؤْتِيَهُ اللَّهُ الْكِتَٰبَ وَالْحُكْمَ وَالنُّبُوَّةَ ثُمَّ يَقُولَ لِلنَّاسِ كُونُوا عِبَادًا لِّي مِن دُونِ اللَّهِ﴾، الآيَةَ [آل عمران: ٧٩].

THE FIFTY-SIXTH ASPECT: Calling the practice of Islam "polytheism", like what He, the Most High, mentioned in His Statement: "It is not for befitting for Allah to give any man the Book, authority, and Prophethood, and then he would say to the people: Be worshippers of me, instead of Allah..." [3:79]

ASPECTS 57-58

DISTORTING & CHANGING THE WORDS OF ALLAH

السَّابِعَةُ وَالخَمْسُونَ: تَحْرِيفُ الكَلِمِ عَنْ مَوَاضِعِهِ.

THE FIFTY-SEVENTH ASPECT: Distorting the Words [of Allah] from their original meanings.

الثَّامِنَةُ وَالخَمْسُونَ: لَيُّ الأَلْسِنَةِ بِالكِتَابِ.

THE FIFTY-EIGHTH ASPECT: Changing the Book by altering its recitation.

ASPECT 59

DISRESPECTFUL & ABUSIVE NAME-CALLING

التَّاسِعَةُ وَالخَمْسُونَ: تَلْقِيبُ أَهْلِ الهُدَى بِالصَّائِبَةِ وَالحَشَوِيَّةِ.

THE FIFTY-NINTH ASPECT: Hurling abusive nicknames at the people of guidance, like: "turncoats" and "worthless people".

ASPECTS 60-61

ATTRIBUTING LIES TO ALLAH & BELYING THE TRUTH

السِّتُّونَ: افْتِرَاءُ الكَذِبِ عَلَى اللهِ.

THE SIXTIETH ASPECT: *Inventing lies and attributing them to Allah.*

الحَادِيَةُ وَالسِّتُّونَ: التَّكْذِيبُ بِالحَقِّ.

THE SIXTY-FIRST ASPECT: *Rejecting the Truth (as if it were lies).*

ASPECTS 62-63

COMPLAINING TO THE RULERS AFTER THEIR DEFEAT

الثَّانِيَةُ وَالسِّتُّونَ: كَوْنُهُمْ إِذَا غُلِبُواْ بِالْحُجَّةِ فَزِعُواْ إِلَى الشَّكْوَى لِلْمُلُوكِ، كَمَا قَالُواْ: ﴿ أَتَذَرُ مُوسَىٰ وَقَوْمَهُۥ لِيُفْسِدُواْ فِى ٱلْأَرْضِ ﴾ [الأعراف: ١٢٧].

THE SIXTY-SECOND ASPECT: *When they were overcome by proofs, they would run off and complain to the rulers, like when they said: "Will you let Moosaa (Moses) and his people cause corruption in the land?"* [7:127]

الثَّالِثَةُ وَالسِّتُّونَ: رَمْيُهُمْ إِيَّاهُمْ بِالْفَسَادِ فِي الْأَرْضِ، كَمَا فِي الْآيَةِ.

THE SIXTY-THIRD ASPECT: *Accusing them (the Prophets and their followers) of causing corruption in the land, as mentioned in the Verse.*

INCITING THE RULER AGAINST THE PEOPLE OF TRUTH

الرَّابِعَةُ وَالسِّتُّونَ: رَمْيُهُمْ إِيَّاهُمْ بِانْتِقَاصِ دِينِ الـــمَلِكِ، كَمَا قَالَ تَعَالَــى:

﴿ وَيَذَرَكَ وَءَالِهَتَكَ ﴾ [الأعراف: ١٢٧]، وَكَمَا قَالَ تَعَالَــى: ﴿ إِنِّ أَخَافُ أَن

يُبَدِّلَ دِينَكُمْ ﴾ [غافر: ٢٦].

THE SIXTY-FOURTH ASPECT: Accusing them (the Prophets and their followers) of criticizing the ruler's religion, as He, the Most High, says: "They abandon you and your deities," [7:127] and as He, the Most High, says: "Verily, I fear that he is going to change your religion." [40:26]

الخَامِسَةُ وَالسِّتُّونَ: رَمْيُهُمْ إِيَّاهُمْ بِانْتِقَاصِ آلِهَةِ المَلِكِ، كَمَا فِي الآيَةِ.

THE SIXTY-FIFTH ASPECT: Accusing them (the Prophets and their followers) of criticizing the ruler's deities, as found in the [same] Verse. (7:127)

ASPECTS 66-67

MORE FALSE CLAIMS AGAINST THE PEOPLE OF TRUTH

السَّادِسَةُ وَالسِّتُّونَ: رَمْيُهُمْ إِيَّاهُمْ بِتَبْدِيلِ الدِّينِ، كَمَا قَالَ تَعَالَى: ﴿ إِنِّي أَخَافُ أَن يُبَدِّلَ دِينَكُمْ أَوْ أَن يُظْهِرَ فِي ٱلْأَرْضِ ٱلْفَسَادَ ﴾ [غافر: ٢٦].

THE SIXTY-SIXTH ASPECT: Accusing them (the Prophets and their followers) of changing the religion, as He, the Most High, says: "Verily, I fear that he is going to change your religion, or bring about corruption in the land." [40:26]

السَّابِعَةُ وَالسِّتُّونَ: رَمْيُهُمْ إِيَّاهُمْ بِانْتِقَاصِ الْمَلِكِ، كَقَوْلِهِمْ: ﴿ وَيَذَرَكَ وَءَالِهَتَكَ ﴾ [الأعراف: ١٢٧].

THE SIXTY-SEVENTH ASPECT: Accusing them (the Prophets and their followers) of criticizing the rulers, like their statement: "They abandon you and your deities." [7:127]

ASPECT 68

CLAIMING TO ACT BY THE TRUTH THEY HAVE

الثَّامِنَةُ وَالسِّتُّونَ: دَعْوَاهُمُ العَمَلِ بِمَا عِنْدَهُمْ مِنَ الحَقِّ، كَقَوْلِهِمْ:

﴿ نُؤْمِنُ بِمَا أُنزِلَ عَلَيْنَا ﴾ [البقرة: ٩١]، مَعَ تَرْكِهِمْ إِيَّاهُ.

THE SIXTY-EIGHTH ASPECT: Claiming to act in accordance with what they have of Truth, like their statement: "We believe in what was revealed to us," [2:91] while they actually abandon it.

ASPECTS 69-70

CHANGING LEGISLATED ACTS OF WORSHIP

التَّاسِعَةُ وَالسِّتُّونَ: الزِّيَادَةُ فِي العِبَادَةِ، كَفِعْلِهِمْ يَوْمَ عَاشُورَاءَ.

THE SIXTY-NINTH ASPECT: Adding onto the [legislated] acts of worship, like what they would do on the Day of 'Aashooraa'.

السَّبْعُونَ: نَقْصُهُمْ مِنْهَا، كَتَرْكِهِمُ الوُقُوفَ بِعَرَفَاتٍ.

THE SEVENTIETH ASPECT: Taking away from that [legislated worship], like when they abandoned standing at 'Arafaat [during the Hajj].

ASPECT 71

ABANDONING RELIGIOUS DUTIES AS AN ACT OF PIETY

الحَادِيَةُ وَالسَّبْعُونَ: تَرْكُهُمُ الوَاجِبَ وَرَعًا.

THE SEVENTY-FIRST ASPECT: Abandoning religious duties out of [assumed] piety.

ASPECTS 72-73

ABANDONING PROVISIONS AS A DISPLAY OF PIETY

الثَّانِيَةُ وَالسَّبْعُونَ: تَعَبُّدُهُمْ بِتَرْكِ الطَّيِّبَاتِ مِنَ الرِّزْقِ .

THE SEVENTY-SECOND ASPECT: Abandoning good things they were provided with as a show of religiosity.

الثَّالِثَةُ وَالسَّبْعُونَ: تَعَبُّدُهُمْ بِتَرْكِ زِينَةِ اللهِ.

THE SEVENTY-THIRD ASPECT: Abandoning nice clothing provided by Allah as a display of religiosity.

ASPECT 74

CALLING TO MISGUIDANCE WITHOUT KNOWLEDGE

الرَّابِعَةُ وَالسَّبْعُونَ: دَعْوَتُهُمُ النَّاسَ إِلَى الضَّلَالِ بِغَيْرِ عِلْمٍ.

THE SEVENTY-FOURTH ASPECT: Calling people to misguidance without knowledge.

ASPECT 75

CALLING TO DISBELIEF WHILST HAVING KNOWLEDGE

الخَامِسَةُ وَالسَّبْعُونَ: دَعْوَتُهُمْ إِيَّاهُمْ إِلَى الكُفْرِ مَعَ العِلْمِ.

THE SEVENTY-FIFTH ASPECT: Calling them to disbelief whilst having knowledge.

ASPECT 76

SERIOUS PLOTS AGAINST THE PEOPLE OF TRUTH

السَّادِسَةُ وَالسَّبْعُونَ: المَكْرُ الكُبَّارُ، كَفِعْلِ قَوْمِ نُوْحٍ.

THE SEVENTY-SIXTH ASPECT: *Scheming very serious plots, like what the people of Nooh (Noah) did.*

ASPECT 77

EVIL SCHOLARS & IGNORANT WORSHIPPERS AS LEADERS

السَّابِعَةُ وَالسَّبْعُونَ: أَنَّ أَئِمَّتَهُمْ إِمَّا عَالِمٌ فَاجِرٌ، وَإِمَّا عَابِدٌ جَاهِلٌ، كَمَا فِي قَوْلِهِ: ﴿ وَقَدْ كَانَ فَرِيقٌ مِّنْهُمْ يَسْمَعُونَ كَلَٰمَ ٱللَّهِ ﴾، إِلَى قَوْلِهِ: ﴿ وَمِنْهُمْ أُمِّيُّونَ لَا يَعْلَمُونَ ٱلْكِتَٰبَ إِلَّآ أَمَانِيَّ ﴾ [البقرة: ٧٥-٧٨].

THE SEVENTY-SEVENTH ASPECT: Their leaders would be either evil scholars or ignorant worshippers, as found in His Statement: "There were some of them who would listen to the Speech of Allah…" up until His Statement: "…And some of them were illiterate, having no knowledge of the Book, just wishful hopes." [2:75-78]

THOSE VERSES

FROM SOORAH AL-BAQARAH [2 : 75-78] *

This passage of the Quran is not from the text of the book, Masaa'il al-Jaahiliyyah.

75. Do you really think they would believe for you, when there were some of them who would listen to the Speech of Allah and then knowingly alter it, after understanding it?

أَفَتَطْمَعُونَ أَن يُؤْمِنُوا لَكُمْ وَقَدْ كَانَ فَرِيقٌ مِّنْهُمْ يَسْمَعُونَ كَلَمَ ٱللَّهِ ثُمَّ يُحَرِّفُونَهُ مِنۢ بَعْدِ مَا عَقَلُوهُ وَهُمْ يَعْلَمُونَ ٧٥

76. When they meet up with those who believe, they say: "We believe." However, when they meet up among themselves in private, they say: "Are you going to tell them about what Allah has made known to you, so they could have an argument against you in front of your Lord?! Do you not have any intellect?!"

وَإِذَا لَقُوا ٱلَّذِينَ ءَامَنُوا قَالُوٓا ءَامَنَّا وَإِذَا خَلَا بَعْضُهُمْ إِلَىٰ بَعْضٍ قَالُوٓا أَتُحَدِّثُونَهُم بِمَا فَتَحَ ٱللَّهُ عَلَيْكُمْ لِيُحَآجُّوكُم بِهِۦ عِندَ رَبِّكُمْ أَفَلَا تَعْقِلُونَ ٧٦

77. Do they not know that Allah does indeed know all they keep secret and all they announce publicly?!

أَوَلَا يَعْلَمُونَ أَنَّ ٱللَّهَ يَعْلَمُ مَا يُسِرُّونَ وَمَا يُعْلِنُونَ ٧٧

78. Some of them are just illiterate, having no knowledge of the Book, just wishful hopes. They do nothing but guess based on conjecture.

وَمِنْهُمْ أُمِّيُّونَ لَا يَعْلَمُونَ ٱلْكِتَبَ إِلَّآ أَمَانِيَّ وَإِنْ هُمْ إِلَّا يَظُنُّونَ ٧٨

ASPECT 78

CLAIMING TO LOVE ALLAH & ABANDONING HIS LEGISLATION

الثَّامِنَةُ وَالسَّبْعُونَ: دَعْوَاهُمْ مَحَبَّةَ اللهِ مَعَ تَرْكِهِمْ شَرْعَهُ، فَطَالَبَهُمُ اللهُ بِقَوْلِهِ:

﴿ قُلْ إِن كُنتُمْ تُحِبُّونَ ٱللَّهَ ﴾ [آل عمران: ٣١].

THE SEVENTY-EIGHTH ASPECT: *Their claim to love Allah while they abandoned His Legislation, so Allah required them [to prove that], with His Statement: "Say: If you truly do love Allah…" [3:31]*

ASPECT 79

HOPING & WISHING FOR FALSE IDEAS

التَّاسِعَةُ وَالسَّبْعُونَ: تَـمَنِّيهِمُ الأَمَانِيَّ الكَاذِبَةَ، كَقَوْلِـهِمْ: ﴿ لَن تَمَسَّنَا ٱلنَّارُ إِلَّا أَيَّامًا مَّعْدُودَةً ﴾ [البقرة: ٨٠]، وَقَوْلِـهِمْ: ﴿ لَن يَدْخُلَ ٱلْجَنَّةَ إِلَّا مَن كَانَ هُودًا أَوْ نَصَرَى ﴾ [البقرة: ١١١].

THE SEVENTY-NINTH ASPECT: Hoping and wishing for false ideas, like when they said: "The Hellfire will not touch us, except for a set number of days." [2:80] And their statement: "None shall enter Paradise other than a Jew or a Christian." [2:111]

ASPECT 80

GRAVES MADE INTO PLACES OF WORSHIP

الثَّمَانُونَ: اتِّخَاذُ قُبُورِ أَنْبِيَائِهِمْ وَصَالِحِيْهِمْ مَسَاجِدَ.

THE EIGHTIETH ASPECT: *Making the graves of their Prophets and righteous people into places of worship.*

ASPECT 81

RELICS OF PROPHETS MADE INTO PLACES OF WORSHIP

الحَادِيَةُ وَالثَّمَانُونَ: اِتِّخَاذُ آثَارِ أَنْبِيَائِهِمْ مَسَاجِدَ، كَمَا ذُكِرَ عَنْ عُمَرَ.

THE EIGHTY-FIRST ASPECT: *Making the relics of their Prophets into places of worship, as was reported from 'Umar.*

ASPECT 82

PLACING LANTERNS AT GRAVESITES

الثَّانِيَةُ وَالثَّمَانُونَ: اتِّخَاذُ السُّرُجِ عَلَى القُبُورِ.

THE EIGHTY-SECOND ASPECT: *Placing lanterns at gravesites.*

ASPECTS 83-84

RITUAL VISITS TO GRAVES & SLAUGHTERING THERE

الثَّالِثَةُ وَالثَّمَانُونَ: اِتِّخَاذُهَا أَعْيَادًا.

THE EIGHTY-THIRD ASPECT: Taking them (the graves) as places of ritual visit.

الرَّابِعَةُ وَالثَّمَانُونَ: الذَّبْحُ عِنْدَ الْقُبُورِ.

THE EIGHTY-FOURTH ASPECT: Slaughtering at gravesites.

ASPECTS 85-86

SEEKING BLESSINGS FROM THE RELICS OF THE ANCIENTS

الـخَامِسَةُ وَالسَّادِسَةُ وَالثَّمَانُونَ: التَّبَرُّكُ بِآثَارِ الـمُعَظَّمِيْنَ، كَدَارِ النَّدْوَةِ، وَافْتِخَارُ مَنْ كَانَتْ تَـحْتَ يَدِهِ بِذَلِكَ، كَمَا قِيْلَ لِـحَكِيْمِ بْنِ حِزَامٍ: بِعْتَ مَكْرَمَةَ قُرَيْشٍ؟! فَقَالَ: ذَهَبَتِ الْمَكَارِمُ إِلَّا التَّقْوَى.

THE EIGHTY-FIFTH AND -SIXTH ASPECTS: Seeking blessings from the relics of their honored leaders, like Daar an-Nadwah, as well as the braggery of those who were in charge of that. This is like when it was said to Hakeem ibn Hizaam, "Have you sold off Quraysh's place of honor?" He replied, "All sources of honor are gone, except piety."

ASPECTS 87-88

BRAGGING ABOUT ANCESTRY & INSULTING PEOPLE'S LINEAGE

السَّابِعَةُ وَالثَّمَانُونَ: الفَخْرُ بِالأَحْسَابِ.

THE EIGHTY-SEVENTH ASPECT: Bragging about ancestry.

الثَّامِنَةُ وَالثَّمَانُونَ: الطَّعْنُ فِي الأَنْسَابِ.

THE EIGHTY-EIGHTH ASPECT: Insulting people's lineage.

ASPECT 89

ATTRIBUTING RAIN TO THE STARS

التَّاسِعَةُ وَالثَّمَانُونَ: الاِسْتِسْقَاءُ بِالأَنْوَاءِ.

THE EIGHTY-NINTH ASPECT: Attributing rain to the stars.

ASPECT 90

WAILING OVER THE DEAD

التِّسْعُونَ: النِّيَاحَةُ عَلَى المَيِّتِ.

THE NINETIETH ASPECT: Wailing over the dead.

ASPECT 91
TRANSGRESSION CONSIDERED HIGHLY VIRTUOUS

الحَادِيَةُ وَالتِّسْعُونَ: أَنَّ أَجَلَّ فَضَائِلِهِمُ البَغْيُ، فَذَكَرَ اللهُ فِيهِ مَا ذَكَرَ.

THE NINETY-FIRST ASPECT: The finest of their [presumed] virtues was transgression, and so Allah mentioned what He mentioned about that.

ASPECT 92

BOASTFULNESS CONSIDERED HIGHLY VIRTUOUS

الثَّانِيَةُ وَالتِّسْعُونَ: أَنَّ أَجَلَّ فَضَائِلِهِمُ الفَخْرُ، وَلَوْ بِحَقٍّ، فَنُهِيَ عَنْهُ.

THE NINETY-SECOND ASPECT: The finest of their [presumed] virtues was boastfulness, even when accurate, yet they were forbidden from [all of] that.

ASPECT 93

BIGOTED PARTISANSHIP CONSIDERED A DUTY

الثَّالِثَةُ وَالتِّسْعُونَ: أَنَّ تَعَصُّبَ الإِنْسَانِ لِطَائِفَتِهِ عَلَى الــحَقِّ

وَالبَاطِلِ أَمْرٌ لَا بُدَّ مِنْهُ عِنْدَهُمْ، فَذَكَرَ اللهُ فِيهِ مَا ذَكَرَ.

THE NINETY-THIRD ASPECT: Bigoted partisanship for their group, whether based on truth or falsehood, was something they considered an absolute duty, so Allah mentioned what He mentioned about that.

ASPECT 94

PEOPLE HELD ACCOUNTABLE FOR THE CRIMES OF OTHERS

الرَّابِعَةُ وَالتِّسْعُونَ: أَنَّ مِنْ دِينِهِمْ أَخْذَ الرَّجُلِ بِجَرِيمَةِ غَيْرِهِ، فَأَنْزَلَ اللهُ:

﴿ وَلَا تَزِرُ وَازِرَةٌ وِزْرَ أُخْرَى ﴾ [الأنعام: ١٦٤].

THE NINETY-FOURTH ASPECT: It was from their way to hold a man accountable for the crimes of others, so Allah sent down: "And no soul bears the burden of another." [6:164]

ASPECT 95

PEOPLE BLAMED FOR THE TRAITS OF OTHERS

الــخَامِسَةُ وَالتِّسْــعُونَ: تَعْيِيـرُ الرَّجُـلِ بِــمَا فِـي غَيْرِهِ،

فَقَالَ: «أَعَيَّرْتَهُ بِأُمِّهِ؟! إِنَّكَ امْرُؤٌ فِيْكَ جَاهِلِيَّةٌ.»

THE NINETY-FIFTH ASPECT: Blaming a man based on characteristics found in others, so he said: "Do you insult him based on [the race of] his mother!? Indeed, you are a man who [still] has [some] Jaahiliyyah within you!"

ASPECT 96

BRAGGERY ABOUT GUARDIANSHIP OF THE KA'BAH

السَّادِسَةُ وَالتِّسْعُونَ: الاِفْتِخَارُ بِوَلاَيَةِ البَيْتِ، فَذَمَّهُمُ اللهُ بِقَوْلِهِ:

﴿ مُسْتَكْبِرِينَ بِهِ سَامِرًا تَهْجُرُونَ ﴾ [المؤمنون: ٦٧].

THE NINETY-SIXTH ASPECT: Bragging about guardianship of the House (the Ka'bah), and so Allah blamed them for that with His Statement: "Arrogant over that, huddling together at night in groups, speaking ill [of the Quran]." [23:67]

ASPECT 97

BRAGGERY ABOUT BEING DESCENDANTS OF PROPHETS

السَّابِعَةُ وَالتِّسْعُونَ: الاِفْتِخَارُ بِكَوْنِهِمْ ذُرِّيَّةَ الأَنْبِيَاءِ، فَأَتَى اللهُ بِقَوْلِهِ:

﴿ تِلْكَ أُمَّةٌ قَدْ خَلَتْ لَهَا مَا كَسَبَتْ ﴾ [البقرة: ١٣٤].

THE NINETY-SEVENTH ASPECT: Bragging about being descendants of the Prophets, so Allah sent them His Statement: "Such was a nation that passed; they shall have what they earned [of good]." [2:134]

ASPECT 98

BRAGGERY ABOUT ONE'S OCCUPATION

الثَّامِنَةُ وَالتِّسْعُونَ: الاِفْتِخَارُ بِالصَّنَائِعِ، كَفِعْلِ أَهْلِ الرِّحْلَتَيْنِ عَلَى أَهْلِ الحَرْثِ.

THE NINETY-EIGHTH ASPECT: Bragging about their occupations, like how those [merchants] who traveled in trade twice a year would boast to the farmers.

ASPECT 99

THE EXAGGERATED STATUS OF WORLDLY MATTERS

التَّاسِعَةُ وَالتِّسْعُونَ: عَظَمَةُ الدُّنْيَا فِي قُلُوبِهِمْ، كَقَوْلِهِمْ: ﴿وَلَوْلَا نُزِّلَ هَذَا الْقُرْءَانُ عَلَى رَجُلٍ مِّنَ الْقَرْيَتَيْنِ عَظِيمٍ﴾ [الزخرف: ٣١].

THE NINETY-NINTH ASPECT: The exaggerated status of worldly matters in their hearts, like their statement: "Had not only this Quran come down upon someone from [either of] the two villages, a great man." [43:31]

106

ASPECT 100

IMPOSING THEIR OPINIONS UPON ALLAH

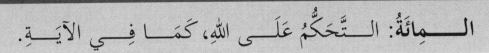

المِـائَةُ: الــتَّحَكُّمُ عَلَــى اللهِ، كَمَــا فِــي الآيَــةِ.

THE ONE HUNDREDTH ASPECT: Subjecting Allah's Rulings to their own personal discretion, as found in the [same] Verse.

ASPECT 101

LOOKING DOWN UPON POOR PEOPLE

الـــحَادِيَةُ بَعْدَ الـــمِائَةِ: ازْدِرَاءُ الْفُقَرَاءِ، فَأَتَاهُمُ اللهُ بِقَوْلِهِ:

﴿ وَلَا تَطْرُدِ ٱلَّذِينَ يَدْعُونَ رَبَّهُم بِٱلْغَدَوٰةِ وَٱلْعَشِيِّ ﴾ [الأنعام: ٥٢].

THE ONE HUNDRED AND FIRST ASPECT: Looking down upon poor people, and so Allah sent them His Statement: "Do not dismiss those who call upon their Lord, morning and evening." [6:52]

ASPECT 102

ACCUSING THE PROPHET'S FOLLOWERS OF INSINCERITY

الثَّانِيَةُ بَعْدَ الْمِائَةِ: رَمْيُهُمْ أَتْبَاعَ الرُّسُلِ بِعَدَمِ الْإِخْلَاصِ وَطَلَبِ الدُّنْيَا، فَأَجَابَهُمْ بِقَوْلِهِ: ﴿ مَا عَلَيْكَ مِنْ حِسَابِهِم مِّن شَيْءٍ ﴾، الْآيَةَ [الأنعام: ٥٢]، وَأَمْثَالَهَا.

THE ONE HUNDRED AND SECOND ASPECT: *Accusing the followers of the Messengers of insincerity and worldly ambitions, to which He responded with His Statement: "Their reckoning is not your responsibility in any way..." [6:52] and its likes.*

DISBELIEVING IN THE ANGELS & MESSENGERS

الثَّالِثَةُ بَعْدَ المِائَةِ: الكُفْرُ بِالمَلَائِكَةِ.

THE ONE HUNDRED AND THIRD ASPECT: Disbelieving in the Angels.

الرَّابِعَةُ بَعْدَ المِائَةِ: الكُفْرُ بِالرُّسُلِ.

THE ONE HUNDRED AND FOURTH ASPECT: Disbelieving in the Messengers.

الخَامِسَةُ بَعْدَ المِائَةِ: الكُفْرُ بِالكُتُبِ.

THE ONE HUNDRED AND FIFTH ASPECT: *Disbelieving in the Books [of Divine Revelation].*

السَّادِسَةُ بَعْدَ المِائَةِ: الإِعْرَاضُ عَمَّا جَاءَ عَنِ اللهِ.

THE ONE HUNDRED AND SIXTH ASPECT: *Turning away from what has come from Allah.*

السَّابِعَةُ بَعْدَ المِائَةِ: الكُفْرُ بِاليَوْمِ الآخِرِ.

THE ONE HUNDRED AND SEVENTH ASPECT: *Disbelieving in the Last Day.*

الثَّامِنَةُ بَعْدَ المِائَةِ: التَّكْذِيْبُ بِلِقَاءِ اللهِ.

THE ONE HUNDRED AND EIGHTH ASPECT: *Rejecting the meeting with Allah [as if it were something untrue].*

ASPECT 109

REJECTING CERTAIN THINGS ABOUT THE LAST DAY

التَّاسِعَةُ بَعْدَ المِائَةِ: التَّكْذِيبُ بِبَعْضِ مَا أَخْبَرَتْ بِهِ الرُّسُلُ عَنِ اليَوْمِ الآخِرِ، كَمَا فِي قَوْلِهِ: ﴿ أُوْلَٰئِكَ ٱلَّذِينَ كَفَرُواْ بِـَٔايَٰتِ رَبِّهِمْ وَلِقَآئِهِۦ ﴾ [الكهف: ١٠٥]، وَمِنْهَا التَّكْذِيبُ بِقَوْلِهِ: ﴿ مَٰلِكِ يَوْمِ ٱلدِّينِ ﴾ [الفاتحة: ٤]، وَقَوْلِهِ: ﴿ لَّا بَيْعٌ فِيهِ وَلَا خُلَّةٌ وَلَا شَفَٰعَةٌ ﴾ [البقرة: ٢٥٤]، وَقَوْلِهِ: ﴿ إِلَّا مَن شَهِدَ بِٱلْحَقِّ وَهُمْ يَعْلَمُونَ ﴾ [الزخرف: ٦٨].

THE ONE HUNDRED AND NINTH ASPECT: Rejecting some of what the Messengers informed us of about the Last Day, like [what is found in] His Statement: "Such are those who disbelieve in the Verses of their Lord and in the meeting with Him." [18:105] From this, as well, was their disbelief in His Statement: "The Owner of the Day of Recompense," [1:4] And His Statement: "There shall be no transaction on that Day, nor any friendship, nor any intercession." [2:254] And His Statement: "Except for those who attest to the Truth, whilst they have knowledge." [46:68]

ASPECT 110

MURDERING THOSE WHO ENJOIN EQUITY

العَاشِرَةُ بَعْدَ المِائَةِ: قَتْلُ الَّذِينَ يَأْمُرُونَ بِالقِسْطِ مِنَ النَّاسِ.

THE ONE HUNDRED AND TENTH ASPECT: Murdering those who enjoin equity.

ASPECT 111

BELIEVING IN MAGICIANS & TRANSGRESSORS

الـحَادِيَةَ عَشْـرَةَ بَعْـدَ الـمِائَةِ: الإِيْـمَانُ بِالـجِبْتِ وَالطَّـاغُوتِ.

THE ONE HUNDRED AND ELEVENTH ASPECT: Believing in magicians and boundless transgressors.

ASPECT 112

PREFERRING POLYTHEISM OVER ISLAM

الثَّانِيَةَ عَشْرَةَ بَعْدَ الْمِائَةِ: تَفْضِيلُ دِيْنِ الْمُشْرِكِيْنَ عَلَى دِيْنِ الْمُسْلِمِيْنَ.

THE ONE HUNDRED AND TWELFTH ASPECT: Preferring the religion of polytheists over the religion of the Muslims.

ASPECT 113

MIXING TRUTH WITH FALSEHOOD

الثَّالِثَةَ عَشْرَةَ بَعْدَ المِائَةِ: لَبْسُ الحَقِّ بِالبَاطِلِ.

THE ONE HUNDRED AND THIRTEENTH ASPECT: Mixing Truth in with falsehood.

ASPECT 114

HIDING THE TRUTH WHEN IT IS KNOWN

الرَّابِعَةَ عَشْرَةَ بَعْدَ الـــمِائَةِ: كِتْمَانُ الـــحَقِّ مَعَ العِلْمِ بِهِ.

THE ONE HUNDRED AND FOURTEENTH ASPECT: Hiding the Truth whilst having knowledge of it.

ASPECT 115

SPEAKING ON BEHALF OF ALLAH WITHOUT KNOWLEDGE

الخَامِسَةَ عَشْرَةَ بَعْدَ المِائَةِ: قَاعِدَةُ الضَّلَالِ، وَهِيَ القَوْلُ عَلَى اللهِ بِلَا عِلْمٍ.

THE ONE HUNDRED AND FIFTEENTH ASPECT, being the central principle of all misguidance: Speaking on behalf of Allah without knowledge.

ASPECT 116

CLEAR SELF-CONTRADICTION AFTER REJECTING TRUTH

السَّادِسَةَ عَشْرَةَ بَعْدَ الـــمِائَةِ: التَّنَاقُضُ الوَاضِحُ لَمَّا كَذَّبُوا بِالـــحَقِّ،

كَمَا قَالَ تَعَالَى: ﴿ بَلْ كَذَّبُوا بِالْحَقِّ لَمَّا جَاءَهُمْ فَهُمْ فِي أَمْرٍ مَرِيجٍ ﴾ [ق: ٥].

THE ONE HUNDRED AND SIXTEENTH ASPECT: Clear self-contradiction after rejecting the Truth, as He, the Most High, says: "Instead, they rejected the Truth when it came to them, and so they are in a state of self-contradiction." [50:5]

ASPECT 117

SELECTIVE BELIEF IN SOME THINGS REVEALED

السَّابِعَةَ عَشْرَةَ بَعْدَ الـمِائَةِ: الإِيْـمَانُ بِبَعْضِ الـمُنَزَّلِ دُوْنَ بَعْضٍ.

THE ONE HUNDRED AND SEVENTEENTH ASPECT: Believing in some of what was revealed, but not all of it.

ASPECT 118

DISTINCTIONS BETWEEN MESSENGERS

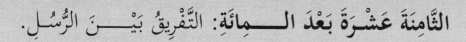

الثَّامِنَةَ عَشْرَةَ بَعْدَ الـــمِائَةِ: التَّفْرِيقُ بَيْــنَ الرُّسُلِ.

THE ONE HUNDRED AND EIGHTEENTH ASPECT: *Making distinctions between the Messengers.*

ASPECT 119

ARGUING OVER MATTERS WITHOUT KNOWLEDGE

التَّاسِعَةَ عَشْرَةَ بَعْدَ الـمِائَةِ: مُخَاصَمَتُهُمْ فِيْمَا لَيْسَ لَـهُمْ بِهِ عِلْمٌ.

THE ONE HUNDRED AND NINETEENTH ASPECT: Arguing over matters about which they have no knowledge.

ASPECT 120

HYPOCRITICALLY CLAIMING TO FOLLOW THE SALAF

العِشْرُونَ بَعْدَ الـمِائَةِ: دَعْوَاهُمُ اتِّبَاعَ السَّلَفِ مَعَ التَّصْرِيْحِ بِـمُخَالَفَتِهِمْ.

THE ONE HUNDRED AND TWENTIETH ASPECT: Claiming to follow [righteous] predecessors whilst flagrantly contradicting them.

ASPECT 121

BLOCKING BELIEVERS FROM FOLLOWING ALLAH'S WAY

الـحَادِيَةُ وَالعِشْـرُونَ بَعْـدَ الـمِائَةِ: صَـدُّهُمْ عَـنْ سَـبِيلِ اللهِ مَنْ آمَـنَ بِـهِ.

THE ONE HUNDRED AND TWENTY-FIRST ASPECT: Blocking those who believe in Allah from following Allah's Path.

ASPECT 122

LOVING DISBELIEF & THE DISBELIEVERS

الثَّانِيَةُ وَالعِشْرُونَ بَعْدَ المِائَةِ: مَوَدَّتُهُمُ الكُفْرَ وَالكَافِرِينَ.

THE ONE HUNDRED AND TWENTY-SECOND ASPECT: Loving disbelief and the disbelievers.

BELIEVING IN SUPERSTITIONS & OMENS, ETC.

الثَّالِثَةُ وَالعِشْرُونَ بَعْدَ الــــمِائَةِ، وَالرَّابِعَةُ، وَالــخَامِسَةُ، وَالسَّادِسَةُ، وَالسَّابِعَةُ، وَالثَّامِنَةُ وَالعِشْرُونَ بَعْدَ الــــمِائَةِ: العِيَافَةُ، وَالطَّرْقُ، وَالطِّيَرَةُ، وَالكَهَانَةُ، وَالتَّحَاكُمْ إِلَــــى الطَّاغُوتِ، وَكَرَاهَةُ التَّزْوِيجِ بَيْـــنَ العِيْدَيْنِ.

THE ONE HUNDRED AND TWENTY-THIRD, -FOURTH, -FIFTH, -SIXTH, -SEVENTH, AND -EIGHTH ASPECTS: Believing in superstitions, omens based on lines drawn in the sand, bird-based omens, and soothsayers, as well as seeking judgments from transgressors and disliking marriages performed between the two 'Eeds.

123. SUPERSTITIONS

124. OMENS BASED ON LINES DRAWN IN THE SAND

125. BIRD-BASED OMENS

126. SOOTHSAYERS

127. SEEKING JUDGMENTS FROM TRANSGRESSORS

128. DISLIKING MARRIAGE BETWEEN THE TWO 'EEDS

ENDING WITH A SUPPLICATION

وَاللهُ أَعْلَمُ، وَصَلَّى اللهُ عَلَى مُحَمَّدٍ وَعَلَى آلِهِ وَصَحْبِهِ وَسَلَّمَ.

And Allah knows best. May Allah raise the rank of Muhammad and his family and companions, and may He grant them all peace.

APPENDIX I

THE COMPLETE TEXT OF THE ENGLISH TRANSLATION

ASPECTS OF THE DAYS OF IGNORANCE

In the Name of Allah, the Most Gracious, the Ever Merciful:

These are affairs in which the Messenger of Allah, may Allah raise his rank and grant him peace, opposed the people of Jaahiliyyah, the People of Scripture as well as the illiterate people [with no book]. These affairs are absolutely necessary for every Muslim to know about.

> An opposite highlights the good of its counterpart,
> As by way of their opposites, things are made clear.

The most crucial and severely dangerous of that is the lack of heart-based faith in what the Messenger came with, may Allah raise his rank and grant him peace. When that is coupled with admiration of the what the people of Jaahiliyyah are/were upon, it is then a complete loss, as He, the Most High, says, "Those who believe in falsehood and disbelieve in Allah, such are the true losers." [29:52]

THE FIRST ASPECT: In their worship, they would direct a share of their supplications and other rites to righteous people (saints), while that was to be for Allah alone. They assumed that such people could intercede for them in front of Allah, and that Allah loved that, and that the righteous also loved that, as He, the Most High, says, "They worship those beside Allah who do not harm them, nor benefit them, saying: These are our intercessors with Allah." [10:18] He, the Most High, also says, "And those who take protectors besides Allah [say]: We do not worship them except that they bring us closer to Allah." [39:3]

This is the greatest issue the Messenger of Allah opposed them in, may Allah raise his rank and grant him peace. In contrast, he came with true sincerity [of Monotheistic worship], and he informed them that this was the true Religion of Allah with which He had sent all Messengers. No deed would ever be accepted, except one done sincerely [for Allah alone]. Additionally, he informed them that whoever did whatever they deemed to be correct (i.e. polytheism) would be barred by Allah from entering Paradise, and the abode of such a person would be Hell.

This is the issue that caused Mankind to split into Muslims and disbelievers. Over it, religious animosity occurs, and jihad (military confrontation) was legislated, as He, the Most High, says: "And fight them until there remains no fitnah (polytheism) and the Religion is entirely for Allah." [8:39]

THE SECOND ASPECT: They were divided in their religion, as He, the Most High, says: "Each party would rejoice with what it had." [30:32] Likewise, in their worldly matters [they were also divided]. They considered this [division] to be correct. In contrast, He (Allah) sent them [orders of] religious solidarity, saying: "He has legislated for you in the Religion what He enjoined upon Nooh (Noah), that which He sent as revelation to you, and that which He enjoined upon Ibraaheem (Abraham), Moosaa (Moses), and 'Eesaa (Jesus): That you establish the Religion and do not be divided within it." [42:13] Also, He, the Most High, says: "Verily, those who split up their religion and became sects, you have nothing at all to do with them." [7:159] He has even forbidden us from resembling them, with His Statement: "Do not be like those who split up and differed after clear evidences came to them." [3:105] Additionally, He has forbidden us from splitting into religious sects with His Statement: "Hold fast to the Rope of Allah, all together, and do not be divided." [3:103]

THE THIRD ASPECT: They considered opposing the leader and not recognizing his authority to be virtuous, while hearing and obeying was considered lowly and disgraceful. So, the Messenger of Allah, may Allah raise his rank and grant him peace, opposed them and ordered [the people] to be patient with the leaders' transgressions. He ordered them to hear, obey, and offer advice. He emphasized this greatly, time and time again.

These three issues have been mentioned all together in what was authentically recorded from him, may Allah raise his rank and grant him peace, in the two Saheeh compilations, that he said: "Verily, Allah is pleased with three things for you: That you worship Him without ascribing any partners to Him at all, that you hold fast to the Rope of Allah, all together, without being divided, and that you advise those whom Allah has placed in charge of your affair." There has never been any deficiency in the people's Religious or worldly affairs, except that it was due to a lapse in these three matters, or in some of them.

THE FOURTH ASPECT: Their religion was based on certain foundations, the greatest of which was blind following. This has always been the core principle of all disbelievers, the first and last of them, as He, the Most High, says: "And thus We sent no warner before you to any nation, except that their extravagant ones said: We found our forefathers upon a way, so we shall remain following in their footsteps." [43:23] He, the Exalted, also says: "When it is said to them: Follow what Allah has revealed! They say: Instead, we shall follow what we found our fathers upon! Even if the Shaytaan were calling them to the torment of the Blazing Fire?!" [31:21] So He delivered His Word to them: "Say: I only admonish you with a single thing – that you stand up [in worship] unto Allah [alone], in groups and individually, and then reflect. There is no demon possessing your companion!" [34:46] And He says: "Follow that which has come down to you from your Lord, and do not follow others less than Him, [taking them] as protectors. Little is the reflection you offer." [7:3]

THE FIFTH ASPECT: From their most central foundations was to be influenced by the majority. They would cite the majority as their evidence for something's correctness. Thus, their proof for something being false would be [merely] its strangeness and the limited number of its supporters. So, He sent them [Revelation proving] the opposite of that and clarified it in more than one passage of the Quran.

THE SIXTH ASPECT: Using ancestors as proofs, like [what is found] in His Statement: "So then what about the first generations?!" [20:51] Also, "We have not heard of this from our forefathers of old!" [23:24]

THE SEVENTH ASPECT: Citing [the behavior of] those given strength in understanding, deeds, authority, wealth, and/or status as evidence. Allah responded to that with His Statement: "And We certainly did enable them in ways We have not enabled you in." [46:26] And His Statement: "They had previously sought victory over those who has disbelieved, yet when there came to them what they were familiar with, they disbelieved in it." [2:89] And His Statement: "They know him as much as they know their own children." [2:146]

THE EIGHTH ASPECT: Trying to disprove something by claiming only the weak and meager follow it, like [what is found in] His Statement: "Shall we believe for you whilst the most meagre [of the people] follow you?!" [26:111] And His Statement: "Are such [poor] people favored by Allah from among us?" To which He responded with His Statement: "Is not Allah most knowledgeable about those who are truly grateful?" [6:53]

THE NINTH ASPECT: Taking evil scholars as role models, and so He sent them His Statement: "O you who have believed! Indeed, there are many priests and monks who devour the people's wealth in falsehood, while they block [them] from the path of Allah." [9:34] And His Statement: "Do not go to extremes in your religion, but just [follow] the Truth. And do not follow the desires of a people who have gone astray long ago, those who misguided many, straying themselves far from the correct path." [5:77]

THE TENTH ASPECT: Claiming that the falsity of a religion is proven by the poor understanding of some of its adherents, and their lack of memorization, like their statement [referring to the followers of the Prophets]: "Those of simple, undeveloped (primitive) opinions." [11:27]

THE ELEVENTH ASPECT: Using false analogies as proofs, like their statement: "You are only human beings like us." [14:10]

THE TWELFTH ASPECT: Rejecting sound analogies. This aspect and the previous one share something in common. They both result from not understanding why issues are similar and should share the same ruling, and why other issues are different and deserve different rulings.

THE THIRTEENTH ASPECT: Having fanaticism towards the scholars and the righteous people, like His Statement: "O People of the Book! Do not go to excesses in your religion! And do not say regarding Allah except the Truth." [4:171]

THE FOURTEENTH ASPECT, which is the underlying principle behind everything which has preceded: Negating [what Allah has affirmed] and affirming [what He has negated]. They merely follow desires and conjecture, while they turn away from what the Messengers came with.

THE FIFTEENTH ASPECT: Excusing themselves from following what Allah had given them, claiming that they do not understand it, like His Statement: "They said: Our hearts are incapable of understanding." [2:88] And: "O Shu'ayb! We do not understand much of what you are saying!" [11:91] So Allah exposed them as liars and clarified that it was because of a seal upon their hearts, a seal that was the result of their own disbelief.

THE SIXTEENTH ASPECT: Replacing what had come to them from Allah with books of magic. Allah mentions this in His Statement: "A group of those given Scripture cast the Book of Allah behind their backs, as if they had no knowledge. Instead, they followed that [magic] which the devils recited during the reign of Sulaymaan (Solomon)." [2:101-102]

THE SEVENTEENTH ASPECT: Attributing their own falsehood to the Prophets, like [what is referred to in] His Statement: "Yet Sulaymaan (Solomon) did not disbelieve," [2:102] and His Statement: "Ibraaheem (Abraham) was not a Jew, nor was he a Christian." [3:67]

THE EIGHTEENTH ASPECT: Contradictory ascriptions, as they would ascribe to Ibraaheem (Abraham), along with their blatant lack of following him.

THE NINETEENTH ASPECT: Reviling righteous people based on the actions of some of those who ascribed to them, like how the Jews reviled 'Eesaa (Jesus), and how both the Jews and Christians reviled Muhammad, may Allah raise his rank and grant him peace.

THE TWENTIETH ASPECT: Their belief that tricks of magicians and similar charlatans were miraculous signs of righteousness, attributing that [idea] to the Prophets, like how they attributed it to Sulaymaan (Solomon), may Allah grant him peace.

THE TWENTY-FIRST ASPECT: They would whistle and clap as worship.

THE TWENTY-SECOND ASPECT: They took their religion as frivolity and amusement.

THE TWENTY-THIRD ASPECT: They were deluded by this worldly life, as they presumed that [receiving] Allah's provisions was proof of His approval [of them and their actions], like their statement: "We have more wealth and children, and we are not going to be punished." [34:35]

THE TWENTY-FOURTH ASPECT: Refusal to embrace the Truth because the weak and meager had already preceded them to it, out of arrogance and disdain. Allah, the Most High, sent down: "Do not dismiss those who call upon their Lord…" [6:52]

THE TWENTY-FIFTH ASPECT: Citing as a proof of something's falsehood that the weak and meager preceded them to it, like [what is found in] His Statement: "Had it been something good, they would not have preceded us to it." [46:11]

THE TWENTY-SIXTH ASPECT: Changing the Book of Allah, after having understood it, whilst they had knowledge.

THE TWENTY-SEVENTH ASPECT: Concocting false scripture and attributing it to Allah, like His Statement: "Woe to those who write the book with their own hands and then say: This is from Allah." [2:79]

THE TWENTY-EIGHTH ASPECT: Refusal to accept anything of the Truth which it is not found with their group, like His Statement: "They said: We only believe in what was sent down to us." [2:91]

THE TWENTY-NINTH ASPECT: Even with that [the previous aspect], they would not really act upon what their group believed anyway, as Allah, the Most High, noted in His

Statement: "Say: Why then have you killed the Prophets of Allah before, if you are indeed believers?" [2:91]

THE THIRTIETH ASPECT, which is from the amazing signs of Allah: After abandoning Allah's Order for unity, they would fall into the differing that Allah forbade them from, each group rejoicing with what they had.

THE THIRTY-FIRST ASPECT, which is also from the most amazing of signs: Their unmatched animosity for the very religion they ascribed to, along with their love of the religion of the disbelievers who despise them and their Prophet. They would love such people with unparalleled love, as they did when the Prophet, may Allah raise his rank and grant him peace, came to them with the Religion of Moosaa (Moses), peace be upon him. They preferred to follow books of magic instead, which was actually from the religion of Pharaoh's people!

THE THIRTY-SECOND ASPECT: Their disbelief in the Truth when it was found with those they did not admire, as Allah, the Most High, says: "The Jews said that the Christians were not upon anything, while the Christians said that the Jews were not upon anything." [2:113]

THE THIRTY-THIRD ASPECT: Rejecting what they had previously acknowledged to be part of their own religion, like what they did regarding Hajj to the House, as Allah, the Most High, says: "Who would be inclined against the Religion of Ibraaheem (Abraham) other than one who makes a fool of himself?" [2:130]

THE THIRTY-FOURTH ASPECT: Every religious sect would claim that it was the saved one, so Allah exposed them as liars with His Statement: "Bring forth your proof if you are indeed truthful." [2:111] Then, He clarified the correct way with His Statement: "Nay! He who submits his face unto Allah, being a person of sincere worship…" [2:112]

THE THIRTY-FIFTH ASPECT: Worshipping with uncovered private parts, as found in His Statement: "When they would commit an obscenity, they would say: We found our fathers doing this, and Allah has ordered us to do it." [7:28]

THE THIRTY-SIXTH ASPECT: Forbidding permissible things as an act of religiosity, whilst also engaging in [forbidden] polytheistic worship.

THE THIRTY-SEVENTH ASPECT: Taking their priests and monks as lords beside Allah, as an act of religiosity.

THE THIRTY-EIGHTH ASPECT: Deviating with regards to the Divine Attributes [of Allah], as He, the Most High, says: "However, you presumed that Allah does not know much of what you do!" [41:22]

THE THIRTY-NINTH ASPECT: Deviating with regards to the Names [of Allah], like His Statement: "And they disbelieve in ar-Rahmaan (the Most Gracious)." [13:30]

THE FORTIETH ASPECT: Absolute denial [of the existence of Allah], similar to the belief of Pharaoh's people.

THE FORTY-FIRST ASPECT: Attributing deficiencies to Him, the Exalted One, like having a child, being needy, and fatigue, while they would exalt their own religious leaders above some of those things!

THE FORTY-SECOND ASPECT: Ascribing partners to Allah in His Dominion and Authority, like the belief of the Zoroastrians.

THE FORTY-THIRD ASPECT: Rejecting Qadr (Divine Decree).

THE FORTY-FOURTH ASPECT: Citing it (Qadr) as a proof Against Allah [absolving themselves of accountability].

THE FORTY-FIFTH ASPECT: Claims of contradiction between Allah's Legislation and His Qadr (Divine Decree).

THE FORTY-SIXTH ASPECT: Speaking ill of time, like their statement: "Nothing causes us to perish other than [the passing of] time." [45:24]

THE FORTY-SEVENTH ASPECT: Ascribing Allah's blessings to others, like His Statement: "They recognize the blessing of Allah, yet they deny it." [16:83]

THE FORTY-EIGHTH ASPECT: Disbelieving in the Verses of Allah.

THE FORTY-NINTH ASPECT: Rejecting some of them.

THE FIFTIETH ASPECT: Their statement: "Allah has not sent down to any human being any revelation at all." [6:91]

THE FIFTY-FIRST ASPECT: Their statement about the Quran: "This is nothing but the word of a human being." [74:25]

THE FIFTY-SECOND ASPECT: Finding fault with the Wisdom of Allah, the Most High.

THE FIFTY-THIRD ASPECT: Using both blatant and hidden trickery to repel what the Messengers have come with, like the Statement of the Most High: "And they plotted, while Allah plotted." [3:54] And His Statement: "A group of the People of the Book said: Believe in the morning in what has been sent down upon those who believe, then disbelieve at the end of the day." [3:72]

THE FIFTY-FOURTH ASPECT: Pretending to acknowledge the Truth in order to plot against it, as He says in the Verse (3:72).

THE FIFTY-FIFTH ASPECT: Partisan-based bigotry for their way, like the Statement of the Most High: "Do not believe except for one who follows your own religion." [3:73]

THE FIFTY-SIXTH ASPECT: Calling the practice of Islam "polytheism", like what He, the Most High, mentioned in His Statement: "It is not for befitting for Allah to give any man the Book, authority, and Prophethood, and then he would say to the people: Be worshippers of me, instead of Allah..." [3:79]

THE FIFTY-SEVENTH ASPECT: Distorting the Words [of Allah] from their original meanings.

THE FIFTY-EIGHTH ASPECT: Changing the Book by altering its recitation.

THE FIFTY-NINTH ASPECT: Hurling abusive nicknames at the people of guidance, like: "turncoats" and "worthless people".

THE SIXTIETH ASPECT: Inventing lies and attributing them to Allah.

THE SIXTY-FIRST ASPECT: Rejecting the Truth (as if it were lies).

THE SIXTY-SECOND ASPECT: When they were overcome by proofs, they would run off and complain to the rulers, like when they said: "Will you let Moosaa (Moses) and his people cause corruption in the land?" [7:127]

THE SIXTY-THIRD ASPECT: Accusing them (the Prophets and their followers) of causing corruption in the land, as mentioned in the Verse (7:127).

THE SIXTY-FOURTH ASPECT: Accusing them (the Prophets and their followers) of criticizing the religion of the ruler, as He, the Most High, says: "They abandon you and your deities," [7:127] and as He, the Most High, says: "Verily, I fear that he is going to change your religion." [40:26]

THE SIXTY-FIFTH ASPECT: Accusing them (the Prophets and their followers) of criticizing the deities of the ruler, as found in the [same] Verse. (7:127)

THE SIXTY-SIXTH ASPECT: Accusing them (the Prophets and their followers) of changing the religion, as He, the Most High, says: "Verily, I fear that he is going to change your religion, or bring about corruption in the land." [40:26]

THE SIXTY-SEVENTH ASPECT: Accusing them (the Prophets and their followers) of criticizing the rulers, like their statement: "They abandon you and your deities." [7:127]

THE SIXTY-EIGHTH ASPECT: Claiming to act in accordance with what they have of Truth, like their statement: "We believe in what was revealed to us," [2:91] while they actually abandon it.

THE SIXTY-NINTH ASPECT: Adding onto the [legislated] acts of worship, like what they would do on the Day of 'Aashooraa'.

THE SEVENTIETH ASPECT: Taking away from that [legislated worship], like when they abandoned standing at 'Arafaat [during the Hajj].

THE SEVENTY-FIRST ASPECT: Abandoning religious duties out of [assumed] piety.

THE SEVENTY-SECOND ASPECT: Abandoning good things they were provided with as a show of religiosity.

THE SEVENTY-THIRD ASPECT: Abandoning nice clothing provided by Allah as a display of religiosity.

THE SEVENTY-FOURTH ASPECT: Calling people to misguidance without knowledge.

THE SEVENTY-FIFTH ASPECT: Calling them to disbelief whilst having knowledge.

THE SEVENTY-SIXTH ASPECT: Scheming very serious plots, like what the people of Nooh (Noah) did.

THE SEVENTY-SEVENTH ASPECT: Their leaders would be either evil scholars or ignorant worshippers, as found in His Statement: "There were some of them who would listen to the Speech of Allah..." up until His Statement: "...And some of them were illiterate, having no knowledge of the Book, just wishful hopes." [2:75-78]

THE SEVENTY-EIGHTH ASPECT: Their claim to love Allah while they abandoned His Legislation, so Allah required them [to prove that], with His Statement: "Say: If you truly do love Allah..." [3:31]

THE SEVENTY-NINTH ASPECT: Hoping and wishing for false ideas, like when they said: "The Hellfire will not touch us, except for a set number of days." [2:80] And their statement: "None shall enter Paradise other than a Jew or a Christian." [2:111]

THE EIGHTIETH ASPECT: Making the graves of their Prophets and righteous people into places of worship.

THE EIGHTY-FIRST ASPECT: Making the relics of their Prophets into places of worship, as was reported from 'Umar.

THE EIGHTY-SECOND ASPECT: Placing lanterns at gravesites.

THE EIGHTY-THIRD ASPECT: Taking them (the graves) as places of ritual visit.

THE EIGHTY-FOURTH ASPECT: Slaughtering at gravesites.

THE EIGHTY-FIFTH AND -SIXTH ASPECTS: Seeking blessings from the relics of their honored leaders, like Daar an-Nadwah, as well as the braggery of those who were in charge of that. This is like when it was said to Hakeem ibn Hizaam, "Have you sold off Quraysh's place of honor?" He replied, "All sources of honor are gone, except piety."

THE EIGHTY-SEVENTH ASPECT: Bragging about ancestry.

THE EIGHTY-EIGHTH ASPECT: Insulting people's lineage.

THE EIGHTY-NINTH ASPECT: Attributing rain to the stars.

THE NINETIETH ASPECT: Wailing over the dead.

THE NINETY-FIRST ASPECT: The finest of their [presumed] virtues was transgression, and so Allah mentioned what He mentioned about that.

THE NINETY-SECOND ASPECT: The finest of their [presumed] virtues was boastfulness, even when accurate, yet they were forbidden from [all of] that.

THE NINETY-THIRD ASPECT: Bigoted partisanship for their group, whether based on truth or falsehood, was something they considered an absolute duty, so Allah mentioned what He mentioned about that.

THE NINETY-FOURTH ASPECT: It was from their way to hold a man accountable for the crimes of others, so Allah sent down: "And no soul bears the burden of another." [6:164]

THE NINETY-FIFTH ASPECT: Blaming a man based on characteristics found in others, so he said: "Do you insult him based on [the race of] his mother!? Indeed, you are a man who [still] has [some] *Jaahiliyyah* within you!"

THE NINETY-SIXTH ASPECT: Bragging about guardianship of the House (the Ka'bah), and so Allah blamed them for that with His Statement: "Arrogant over that, huddling together at night in groups, speaking ill [of the Quran]." [23:67]

THE NINETY-SEVENTH ASPECT: Bragging about being descendants of the Prophets, so Allah sent them His Statement: "Such was a nation that passed; they shall have what they earned [of good]." [2:134]

THE NINETY-EIGHTH ASPECT: Bragging about their occupations, like how those [merchants] who traveled in trade twice a year would boast to the farmers.

THE NINETY-NINTH ASPECT: The exaggerated status of worldly matters in their hearts, like their statement: "Had not only this Quran come down upon someone from [either of] the two villages, a great man." [43:31]

THE ONE HUNDREDTH ASPECT: Subjecting Allah's Rulings to their own personal discretion, as found in the [same] Verse. (43:31)

THE ONE HUNDRED AND FIRST ASPECT: Looking down upon poor people, and so Allah sent them His Statement: "Do not dismiss those who call upon their Lord, morning and evening." [6:52]

THE ONE HUNDRED AND SECOND ASPECT: Accusing the followers of the Messengers of insincerity and worldly ambitions, to which He responded with His Statement: "Their reckoning is not your responsibility in any way..." [6:52] and its likes.

THE ONE HUNDRED AND THIRD ASPECT: Disbelieving in the Angels.

THE ONE HUNDRED AND FOURTH ASPECT: Disbelieving in the Messengers.

THE ONE HUNDRED AND FIFTH ASPECT: Disbelieving in the Books [of Divine Revelation].

THE ONE HUNDRED AND SIXTH ASPECT: Turning away from what has come from Allah.

THE ONE HUNDRED AND SEVENTH ASPECT: Disbelieving in the Last Day.

THE ONE HUNDRED AND EIGHTH ASPECT: Rejecting the meeting with Allah [as if it were something untrue].

THE ONE HUNDRED AND NINTH ASPECT: Rejecting some of what the Messengers informed us of about the Last Day, like [what is found in] His Statement: "Such are those who disbelieve in the Verses of their Lord and in the meeting with Him." [18:105] From this, as well, was their disbelief in His Statement: "The Owner of the Day of Recompense," [1:4] And His Statement: "There shall be no transaction on that Day, nor any friendship, nor any intercession." [2:254] And His Statement: "Except for those who attest to the Truth, whilst they have knowledge." [46:68]

THE ONE HUNDRED AND TENTH ASPECT: Murdering those who enjoin equity.

THE ONE HUNDRED AND ELEVENTH ASPECT: Believing in magicians and boundless transgressors.

THE ONE HUNDRED AND TWELFTH ASPECT: Preferring the religion of polytheists over the religion of the Muslims.

THE ONE HUNDRED AND THIRTEENTH ASPECT: Mixing Truth in with falsehood.

THE ONE HUNDRED AND FOURTEENTH ASPECT: Hiding the Truth whilst having knowledge of it.

THE ONE HUNDRED AND FIFTEENTH ASPECT, being the central principle of all misguidance: Speaking on behalf of Allah without knowledge.

THE ONE HUNDRED AND SIXTEENTH ASPECT: Clear self-contradiction after rejecting the Truth, as He, the Most High, says: "Instead, they rejected the Truth when it came to them, and so they are in a state of self-contradiction." [50:5]

THE ONE HUNDRED AND SEVENTEENTH ASPECT: Believing in some of what was revealed, but not all of it.

THE ONE HUNDRED AND EIGHTEENTH ASPECT: Making distinctions between the Messengers.

THE ONE HUNDRED AND NINETEENTH ASPECT: Arguing over matters about which they have no knowledge.

THE ONE HUNDRED AND TWENTIETH ASPECT: Claiming to follow [righteous] predecessors whilst flagrantly contradicting them.

THE ONE HUNDRED AND TWENTY-FIRST ASPECT: Blocking those who believe in Allah from following Allah's Path.

THE ONE HUNDRED AND TWENTY-SECOND ASPECT: Loving disbelief and the disbelievers.

THE ONE HUNDRED AND TWENTY-THIRD, -FOURTH, -FIFTH, -SIXTH, -SEVENTH, AND -EIGHTH ASPECTS: Believing in superstitions, omens based on lines drawn in the sand, bird-based omens, and soothsayers, as well as seeking judgments from transgressors and disliking marriages performed between the two 'Eeds.

And Allah knows best. May Allah raise the rank of Muhammad and his family and companions, and may He grant them all peace.

Answer the following multiple-choice questions about the introduction and the first 14 aspects of *Jaahiliyyah* from the book, *Aspects of the Days of Ignorance*.

1. The author of the book, *Masaa'il al-Jaahiliyyah*, is:

    A Ibn Taymiyah
    B Muhammad ibn 'Abdil-Wahhaab
    C 'Abdur-Rahmaan ibn Hasan
    D 'Abdul-'Azeez ibn Baaz

2. The total number of issues, or *mas'alahs* (aspects), mentioned in the book is:

    A more than 100
    B more than 210
    C 67
    D 92

3. In his introduction, what is the reason provided by the author for studying these evil, negative things?

    A Things are made clear by understanding their opposites, comparatively.
    B It is beneficial to love evil things in some situations.
    C The People of the Book ignored them, therefore we should focus on them.
    D These issues have been studied traditionally for over 1000 years.

4. In his introduction, what combination of things does the author describe as a "total loss"?

    A atheism, polytheism, and speaking without knowledge
    B innovation and sinful behavior
    C these aspects from the days of *Jaahiliyyah* and hypocrisy in action
    D disbelief and fondness of what the people of *Jaahiliyyah* were upon

5. In his introduction, which two main groups of people does the author refer to as people of *Jaahiliyyah*?

    A pre-Islamic Arabs and non-Arabs
    B Jews and Christians
    C the People of the Book and the unlettered Arabs before Islam
    D atheists and pre-Islamic Arabs

6. The people of *Jaahiliyyah* generally thought that calling upon saints was:

    A impermissible polytheism

    B something which Allah was pleased with

    C allowed, because those saints had more power and capability than Allah

    D something the saints themselves hated

7. The people of *Jaahiliyyah* were divided into religious factions, so Allah:

    A allowed them to continue in that, so long as they were sincere in worship

    B discouraged that, but did not forbid it absolutely

    C encouraged them to continue in that

    D forbade that and ordered them with religious solidarity upon the Truth

8. What is true about *Jaahiliyyah* and obedience to the ruler?

    A They used to obey the ruler in *Jaahiliyyah*, until Allah encouraged rebellion.

    B They used to disregard the ruler in *Jaahiliyyah*.

    C They considered obedience to the rulers a great honor and high virtue.

    D The rulers of *Jaahiliyyah* were righteous and pious.

9. What does the author name as "the core principle of all disbelievers, the first and last of them"?

    A rebellion against authority figures

    B *shirk* (polytheism)

    C splitting into religious factions

    D *taqleed* (blind following)

10. The People of *Jaahiliyyah* considered the Truth to be in agreement with:

    A the majority

    B the ways of their ancestors

    C the people of social status and prosperity

    D all of the above

APPENDIX III

CHECK YOUR UNDERSTANDING OF ASPECTS 15–42

Answer the following multiple-choice questions about Aspects 15-42 from the book,
Aspects of the Days of Ignorance.

1. Shu'ayb's people claimed they could not understand his words. Allah clarified that:

      A it was because of Shu'ayb's shyness and they should be patient.
      B it was the result of a seal placed over their hearts.
      C Shu'ayb was forbidden from speaking for a period of three days.
      D they really did understand what he was saying.

2. According to the author's 17th point, the people of *Jaahiliyyah* attributed false things to Prophets, like how they attributed _____ to Sulaymaan.

      A magic
      B being a Jew
      C atheism
      D lying

3. According to the author's 20th point, the people of *Jaahiliyyah* considered illusionary magical tricks to be:

      A similar to the magic of Pharaoh
      B revelation
      C proof of prophethood
      D miracles of the righteous

4. What two things did Allah blame the people of *Jaahiliyyah* for doing as worship at the Ka'bah in Makkah specifically?

      A dancing and singing
      B reciting poetry and engaging in trade
      C clapping and whistling
      D praying in the wrong direction and nakedness

5. What error(s) did the people of *Jaahiliyyah* make in how they understood status and worldly prosperity?

      A They considered someone's low status to be a proof against his religion.
      B They would not embrace the Truth if the meager preceded them to it.
      C They considered their own prosperity to be a proof of their correctness.
      D all of the above

6. How did the people of *Jaahiliyyah* display bigoted partisanship?

    A They would only embrace something of the Truth if their group already had it.

    B They would embrace the Truth no matter who had it.

    C They never embraced anything of the Truth, ever.

    D They required their leaders to embrace the Truth and leave their old ways.

7. In the 29th point, the author mentions as a proof that the people of *Jaahiliyyah* did not really act upon the aspects of the Truth they claimed to ascribe to anyway:

    A They buried their Prophets inside the Ka'bah.

    B They buried their daughters alive.

    C They would try to kill their own Prophets.

    D They gave copies of the Torah to the pagan Romans and Persians.

8. In the author's 31st point, what example is cited to show how the people of *Jaahiliyyah* embraced the religion of their enemies whilst rejecting the Religion of their own Prophets?

    A Pagans in Makkah wore crosses around their necks at Christian celebrations.

    B The Jews of Madeenah followed books of magic and rejected Muhammad.

    C Pharaoh's people worshipped him and called Moosaa a magician.

    D Christians in Yemen would place the Torah over the Bible in some ceremonies.

9. The people of *Jaahiliyyah* were religiously divided, yet each faction claimed to be the saved sect. About this, the author commented:

    A This proves that no Muslim can ever claim to be from the "saved sect".

    B Religious differing is going to happen, and it is something we have to accept.

    C No one can ever know who the "saved sect" is.

    D Allah rejected their claim and challenged them to bring forth their proof.

10. Which of the following things does Allah blame the people of *Jaahiliyyah* for including in their acts of worship?

    A nakedness

    B forbidding permissible things

    C taking religious leaders as lords beside Allah

    D all of the above

APPENDIX IV

CHECK YOUR UNDERSTANDING OF ASPECTS 43-67

Answer the following multiple-choice questions about aspects 43-67 from the book,
Aspects of the Days of Ignorance.

1. Which of the following violations did the people of *Jaahiliyyah* commit regarding *Qadar*?
   - A They flat-out rejected it.
   - B They claimed contradictions between *Qadar* and Allah's legislative orders.
   - C They claimed they were excused from their disbelief because of the *Qadar*.
   - D all of the above

2. Which Verse(s) does the author cite as a proof that the people of Jaahiliyyah would say abusive things about time? *(The answer is the Verse which means...)*
   - A "Nothing causes us to perish other than [the passing of] time." [45:24]
   - B "They recognize the blessing of Allah, yet they deny it." [16:83]
   - C "By the passing of time, all of Mankind is in loss..." [Soorah al-'Asr]
   - D a verse from the Old Testament

3. Which of the following stances on the Quran were held by the people of *Jaahiliyyah*?
   - A They disbelieved in its Verses.
   - B They claimed no revelation had come to any human being.
   - C They claimed it was just the speech of a human being.
   - D all of the above

4. What is true about the Jews and Christians who accepted Islam?
   - A None of them did that sincerely; it was always a trick to lead people astray.
   - B Actually no Jews or Christians ever accepted Islam.
   - C Some of them would accept Islam and then leave it, to lead people astray.
   - D Every Jew and Christian who openly accepted Islam became a true believer.

5. The author quotes the Verse which means, "Do not believe except for one who follows your own religion," [3:73] in order to prove which point?
   - A Following the Truth includes bigoted partisanship sometimes.
   - B Many of the people of Jaahiliyyah were sincere and obedient.
   - C Most of the people of Jaahiliyyah were not Arabs.
   - D People in Jaahiliyyah behaved with bigoted partisanship.

6. Allah revealed the Verse which means, "It is not for befitting for Allah to give any man the Book, authority, and Prophethood, and then he would say to the people: Be worshippers of me, instead of Allah..." [3:79] as a response to which claim(s) made by the people of *Jaahiliyyah*?

    A Prophets only want governmental authority.
    B Islam is actually *shirk* (polytheism).
    C Allah never sent down any revelation.
    D all of the above

7. The people of *Jaahiliyyah* unjustly hurled abusive nick-names at the followers of the Truth. What two examples does the author provide for this in his 59th point?

    A "turncoats" and "worthless people"
    B "fools" and "idiots"
    C "murderers" and "thieves"
    D "liars" and "betrayers"

8. What action of Pharaoh and his people is cited as a trait of the people of *Jaahiliyyah*?

    A reporting the people of Truth to the authorities after being overcome by proofs
    B inciting the rulers against the followers of the Prophets
    C claiming that the followers of the Prophets are causing corruption in the land
    D all of the above

9. Who is being quoted in the Verse [40:26] which means, "Verily, I fear that he is going to change your religion, or bring about corruption in the land..."?

    A Pharaoh said this to his people.
    B Quraysh said this in their private gatherings.
    C Those who plotted against Jesus said this to the Jews.
    D The people of Egypt said this to Pharaoh.

10. What is true about the behavior of Pharaoh and his people as it relates to the overall content and goal of the book, *Aspects of the Days of Ignorance*?

    A Pharaoh's era was actually before *Jaahiliyyah*, so their behavior was irrelevant.
    B Their behavior was not cited in the book, but it should have been.
    C Pharaoh accepted Islam and then rejected it as a plot to lead people astray.
    D Their behavior is very relevant to the topic and cited often in the book.

APPENDIX V

CHECK YOUR UNDERSTANDING OF ASPECTS 68–113

Answer the following multiple-choice questions about aspects 68-113 from the book, *Aspects of the Days of Ignorance*.

1. In the 69th aspect, the author mentions that the people of *Jaahiliyyah* added onto the [legislated] acts of worship. Which example(s) of that behavior does he provide?

       A what they would do on the Day of *'Aashooraa'*
       B what they would do on the Day of *'Arafaat*
       C requiring people to be naked at the Ka'bah for worship
       D all of the above

2. In the 70th aspect, the author mentions that the people of *Jaahiliyyah* removed some [legislated] acts of worship. Which example of that behavior does he provide?

       A They stopped praying at the correctly legislated times.
       B They refused to sacrifice any animals anywhere in Makkah.
       C They abandoned standing at *'Arafaat* [during the *Hajj*].
       D They refused to fast or pay *zakaat* for many years.

3. In the 77th aspect, the author explains that the people of Jaahiliyyah would have leaders who were either _____ or _____.

       A evil scholars; ignorant scholars
       B ignorant worshippers; evil merchants
       C arrogant poets; greedy scholars
       D evil scholars; ignorant worshippers

4. Allah requires all those who claim to love Him to:

       A call forth their witnesses
       B make a written record of that claim and have it witnessed
       C follow His Messenger (may Allah raise his rank and grant him peace)
       D all of the above

5. In the 79th aspect, the author explains that hoping and wishing for false ideas was from the behavior of the people of *Jaahiliyyah*. Which Verse(s) does he cite to prove that?

       A "The Hellfire will not touch us, except for a set number of days." [2:80]
       B "None shall enter Paradise other than a Jew or a Christian." [2:111]
       C "We believe in what was revealed to us..." [2:91]
       D both A and B

6. Which of the following errors relative to graves was cited by the author as behavior of the people of *Jaahiliyyah*?

    A They took graves as masjids and illuminated them with lanterns.
    B They sacrificed animals at graves.
    C They made graveyards places of ritual visit.
    D all of the above

7. The author mentions that when Hakeem ibn Hizaam sold off the building, *Daar an-Nadwah*, some people objected, saying: "Have you sold off Quraysh's place of honor!?" What was his response?

    A "*Daar an-Nadwah* was merely a place of plotting and scheming."
    B "All sources of honor are gone, except piety."
    C "Why would I not sell off the property of traitors?"
    D Out of respect for Quraysh's elders, he remained silent.

8. In the 94th aspect, the author mentions that the people of *Jaahiliyyah* would hold a man accountable for the crimes of others, so Allah sent down (what means):

    A "And no soul bears the burden of another..." [6:164]
    B "Every soul shall taste death..." [29:57]
    C "Such are those who disbelieve in the Verses of their Lord..." [18:105]
    D "Their reckoning is not your responsibility in any way..." [6:52]

9. About which behavior from *Jaahiliyyah* did the Prophet (may Allah raise his rank and grant him peace) once rebuke a Companion over, saying (what means): "You are a man who [still] has [some] *Jaahiliyyah* within you!"

    A astrology
    B racism
    C superstitions
    D swearing by one's father

10. Complete the statement of the author, from the 102nd aspect: "Accusing the followers of the Messengers of _____, to which He responded with His Statement: 'Their reckoning is not your responsibility in any way...' [6:52] and its likes."

    A transgression and injustice
    B lies and trickery
    C greed and arrogance
    D insincerity and worldly ambitions

Answer the following multiple-choice questions about the final fifteen aspects of *Jaahiliyyah* from the book, *Aspects of the Days of Ignorance*.

1. The author calls this 115th aspect, "The central principle of all misguidance."

    A ignorance of Allah's Revelation
    B speaking on behalf of Allah without knowledge
    C following the ways of the ancestors
    D arrogance

2. In the 116th aspect, the author notes that the *Jaahiliyyah* crime of _____ necessarily leads to obvious self-contradiction.

    A rejecting the Truth
    B racism
    C unjustifiable murder
    D adultery

3. How did the people of *Jaahiliyyah* make impermissible distinctions between the Messengers?

    A They would believe in some of them and disbelieve in others.
    B They would claim that Allah gave some of them ranks over others.
    C They would claim that some of them were Prophets, but not Messengers.
    D all of the above

4. What is true about omens derived from lines drawn in the sand?

    A They are forbidden forms of polytheism.
    B They were practiced by the people of Jaahiliyyah.
    C They were one form of many different types of superstitions.
    D all of the above

5. In the final 128th aspect, what permissible thing(s) did the author mention that the people of *Jaahiliyyah* would avoid between the two 'Eeds?

    A marriage
    B divorce
    C major business deals
    D all of the above

APPENDIX VII

TEST YOUR UNDERSTANDING OF THE BOOK

Answer the following multiple-choice questions about the book, *Aspects of the Days of Ignorance*.

1. The author of the book, *Masaa'il al-Jaahiliyyah*, is:
   - A Muhammad ibn Saalih al-'Uthaymeen
   - B 'Ubayd al-Jaabiree
   - C Ibn Qayyim al-Jowziyyah
   - D Muhammad ibn 'Abdil-Wahhaab at-Tameemee

2. In his introduction, what is the reason provided by the author for studying these evil, negative things?
   - A It is sometimes allowed to love evil things in some situations.
   - B Things are made clear by understanding their opposites, comparatively.
   - C The People of the Book ignored them, therefore we should focus on them.
   - D all of the above

3. In his introduction, what combination of things does the author describe as a "total loss"?
   - A atheism, polytheism, and speaking without knowledge
   - B innovation and political ambitions
   - C disbelief and fondness of what the people of Jaahiliyyah were upon
   - D all of the above

4. Who are the two main groups of people referred to by the author in his introduction as "The people of *Jaahiliyyah*"?
   - A the Jews and Christians
   - B the People of the Book and the illiterate Arabs before Islam
   - C philosophical atheists and pre-Islamic Arabs
   - D pre-Islamic Arabs and Roman non-Arabs

5. The people of *Jaahiliyyah* generally considered calling upon saints to be:
   - A an unacceptable act of flagrant polytheism
   - B something which Allah was pleased with
   - C allowed, because those saints had more power and capability than Allah
   - D something even the saints themselves hated

6. In his discussion of the fourth aspect, what does the author cite as: "The core principle of all disbelievers, the first and last of them..."?

    A *bid'ah* (Innovation)
    B splitting into religious sects
    C *taqleed* (blind following)
    D rebellion against rulers

7. According to the author's 17ᵗʰ point, the people of *Jaahiliyyah* attributed false things to Prophets, like how they attributed magic to _____.

    A Daawood
    B Moosaa
    C Sulaymaan
    D Nooh

8. According to the author's 20ᵗʰ point, the people of *Jaahiliyyah* considered illusionary magical tricks to be:

    A proofs of righteousness
    B revelation
    C qualities of a true leader
    D blameworthy paganism

9. What two things did Allah blame the people of *Jaahiliyyah* for doing as worship at the Ka'bah in Makkah specifically?

    A dancing and singing
    B reciting poetry and engaging in trade
    C reading the Torah and dancing
    D clapping and whistling

10. How did the people of *Jaahiliyyah* display bigoted partisanship?

    A They would only embrace a matter of Truth if their group already had it.
    B They would embrace all matters of Truth no matter who had them first.
    C They required their leaders to embrace the Truth and leave their old ways.
    D They never embraced anything of the Truth, ever.

11. In the author's 29ᵗʰ aspect, he mentioned that the people of *Jaahiliyyah* did not really act upon the aspects of the Truth they claimed to ascribe to anyway. What example did he provide for this behavior?

    A They gave copies of the Bible to the pagan Romans and Persians.
    B They buried their ancestors inside the Ka'bah.
    C They buried their own children alive.
    D They would try to kill their own Prophets.

12. The people of *Jaahiliyyah* were religiously divided, yet each faction claimed to be the saved sect. About this, the author commented:

    A Religious differing is going to happen, and it is something we have to accept.
    B This proves that no one can ever claim to be from the "saved sect".
    C No one could ever know who the "saved sect" is.
    D none of the above

13. Which of the following violations did the people of *Jaahiliyyah* commit regarding the Divine Decree (*Qadar*) of Allah?

    A They flat-out rejected it.
    B They claimed there were no contradictions between *Qadar* and Allah's orders.
    C They simply affirmed *Qadar* without delving into its specific details.
    D all of the above

14. Which of the following stances on the Quran were held by the people of *Jaahiliyyah*?

    A They believed in its Verses.
    B They claimed no revelation had been revealed to any human being.
    C They claimed it was the Speech of Allah, not a created thing.
    D all of the above

15. The author quotes the Verse which means, "Do not believe except for one who follows your own religion," [3:73] in order to prove which point?

    A Most of the people of Jaahiliyyah were not Arabs.
    B Following the Truth includes bigoted partisanship sometimes.
    C Many of the people of Jaahiliyyah were sincere and obedient.
    D People in Jaahiliyyah displayed bigoted partisanship.

16. Allah revealed the Verse which means, "It is not for befitting for Allah to give any man the Book, authority, and Prophethood, and then he would say to the people: Be worshippers of me, instead of Allah..." [3:79] as a response to which claim(s) made by the people of *Jaahiliyyah*?

    A Prophets only want money.
    B Allah never sent down any revelation.
    C Islam is actually *shirk* (polytheism).
    D all of the above

17. Which action of Pharaoh and his people is cited as an evil trait of *Jaahiliyyah*?

    A reporting the people of Truth to the authorities after being overcome by proofs
    B encouraging the rulers to follow the Prophets
    C claiming that the followers of the Prophets are spreading righteousness
    D none of the above

18. What is true about the behavior of Pharaoh and his people as it relates to the overall content and theme of the book, *Aspects of the Days of Ignorance*?

    A Their era was actually before *Jaahiliyyah*, so their behavior was irrelevant.
    B Pharaoh accepted Islam and then rejected it, in order to mislead people.
    C Their behavior was not cited in the book at all, but it should have been.
    D Their behavior is very relevant to the topic and cited much in the book.

19. In the 69th aspect, the author mentions that the people of *Jaahiliyyah* added on to the [legislated] acts of worship. Which example(s) of that behavior does he provide?

    A what they would do on the Day of *'Arafaat*
    B what they would do on the Day of *'Aashooraa'*
    C requiring people to purchase their clothes for worship in Makkah
    D fasting during hot days, without taking any shade

20. In the 77ᵗʰ aspect, the author explains that the people of Jaahiliyyah would have leaders who were either _____ or _____.

    A evil scholars; greedy merchants
    B evil scholars; ignorant worshippers
    C ignorant worshippers; evil merchants
    D arrogant poets; greedy scholars

21. Allah requires all those who claim to love Him to:

    A call forth their witnesses
    B make a written record of that claim and have it witnessed
    C follow His Messenger (may Allah raise his rank and grant him peace)
    D all of the above

22. Which of the following errors relative to graves was cited by the author as behavior of the people of *Jaahiliyyah*?

    A They took graves as masjids.
    B They sacrificed animals at graves.
    C They made graveyards places of ritual visit, and placed lanterns there.
    D all of the above

23. A man was blamed for selling off a prized location of honor. He responded: *"All sources of honor are gone, except piety."* Who said this? And what was that special location?

    A Aboo Hurayrah said this about the birthplace of 'Umar ibn al-Khattaab.
    B Hakeem ibn Hizaam said this about *Daar an-Nadwah* in Makkah.
    C 'Abdullaah ibn 'Amr said this about the houses closest to the Ka'bah.
    D Salmaan al-Faarisee said this about the entire city of Bukhara.

24. About which behavior left over from *Jaahiliyyah* did the Prophet (may Allah raise his rank and grant him peace) once rebuke a Companion over, saying (what means): "You are a man who [still] has [some] *Jaahiliyyah* within you!"

    A listening to a soothsayer (but not believing in his predictions)
    B lying in one's oaths
    C a racial slur made against another Companion
    D raising prices in an auction without intending to actually buy anything

25. The author calls this 115ᵗʰ aspect, "The central principle of all misguidance."

    A ignorance of Allah's Revelation
    B following the ways of the ancestors
    C arrogance
    D speaking on behalf of Allah without knowledge

APPENDIX VIII

CHECK YOUR MEMORIZATION OF ASPECTS 1-14

Fill in the missing words and phrases from the first part of the Arabic text of the book, *Aspects of the Days of Ignorance*, from the Introduction to the 14ᵗʰ Aspect.

هَذِهِ أُمُورٌ خَالَفَ فِيهَا رَسُولُ اللهِ صَلَّى اللهُ عَلَيْهِ وَسَلَّمَ أَهْلَ الْـجَاهِلِيَّةِ _____

وَ_____ ، مِمَّا لَا غِنَى لِلْمُسْلِمِ عَنْ _____ .

فَالضِّدُّ يُظْهِرُ حُسْنَهُ الضِّدُّ   وَبِضِدِّهَا _____

الْـمَسْأَلَةُ _____ : أَنَّـهُمْ يَتَعَبَّدُونَ بِإِشْرَاكِ الصَّالِـحِينَ فِي _____

وَ_____ ، يُرِيدُونَ شَفَاعَتَهُمْ عِنْدَ اللهِ لِظَنِّهِمْ أَنَّ اللهَ _____ ،

وَأَنَّ الصَّالِـحِينَ يُـحِبُّونَهُ، كَمَا قَالَ تَعَالَى: ﴿ وَيَعْبُدُونَ مِن دُونِ ٱللَّهِ _____

_____ وَيَقُولُونَ هَٰؤُلَآءِ شُفَعَٰٓؤُنَا عِندَ ٱللَّهِ ﴾ [يونس: ١٨]، وَقَالَ تَعَالَى:

﴿ وَٱلَّذِينَ ٱتَّخَذُواْ مِن دُونِهِۦٓ أَوْلِيَآءَ _____ ﴾ [الزمر: ٣].

وَهَذِهِ الْـمَسَائِلُ الثَّلَاثُ هِيَ الَّتِي جَمَعَ بَيْنَهَا فِيمَا صَحَّ عَنْهُ صَلَّى اللهُ عَلَيْهِ وَسَلَّمَ فِي

الصَّحِيْحَيْنِ أَنَّهُ قَالَ: «إِنَّ اللهَ يَرْضَى لَكُمْ ثَلَاثًا: _____

_____ »، وَلَـمْ يَقَعْ

خَلَلٌ فِي دِينِ النَّاسِ وَدُنْيَاهُمْ إِلَّا _____ .

الرَّابِعَةُ: أَنَّ دِينَهُمْ مَبْنِيٌّ عَلَى أُصُولٍ

_____ ، كَمَا قَالَ تَعَالَى: ﴿ وَكَذَٰلِكَ مَا أَرْسَلْنَا مِن قَبْلِكَ فِي قَرْيَةٍ مِّن

نَّذِيرٍ إِلَّا _____ ﴾

[الزخرف: ٢٣]، وَقَالَ تَعَالَى: ﴿ وَإِذَا قِيلَ لَهُمُ ٱتَّبِعُوا مَا أَنزَلَ ٱللَّهُ قَالُوا بَلْ نَتَّبِعُ مَا

وَجَدْنَا عَلَيْهِ ءَابَاءَنَا _____ ﴾

[لقمان: ٢١]، فَأَتَاهُمْ بِقَوْلِهِ: ﴿ قُلْ إِنَّمَا أَعِظُكُم بِوَٰحِدَةٍ أَن تَقُومُوا لِلَّهِ مَثْنَىٰ وَفُرَٰدَىٰ

ثُمَّ تَتَفَكَّرُوا مَا بِصَاحِبِكُم مِّن جِنَّةٍ ﴾، الآيَةَ [سبأ: ٤٦]، وَقَوْلِهِ:

﴿ _____ ﴾ [الأعراف: ٣].

التَّاسِعَةُ: _____ ، فَأَتَى بِقَوْلِهِ: ﴿ يَٰٓأَيُّهَا ٱلَّذِينَ ءَامَنُوٓا إِنَّ

كَثِيرًا مِّنَ ٱلْأَحْبَارِ وَٱلرُّهْبَانِ لَيَأْكُلُونَ أَمْوَٰلَ ٱلنَّاسِ بِٱلْبَٰطِلِ وَيَصُدُّونَ عَن سَبِيلِ

ٱللَّهِ ﴾ [التوبة: ٣٤]، وَقَوْلِهِ: ﴿

_____ ﴾ [المائدة: ٧٧].

الثَّالِثَةَ عَشْرَةَ: الغُلُوُّ فِي العُلَمَاءِ وَالصَّالِحِينَ، كَقَوْلِهِ: ﴿

_____ ﴾ [النساء: ١٧١].

الرَّابِعَةَ عَشْرَةَ: أَنَّ كُلَّ مَا تَقَدَّمَ مَبْنِيٌّ عَلَى قَاعِدَةٍ وَهِيَ _____ ، فَيَتَّبِعُونَ

_____ وَ_____ ، وَيُعْرِضُونَ عَمَّا جَاءَتْ _____ .

APPENDIX IX

CHECK YOUR MEMORIZATION OF ASPECTS 15-42

Fill in the missing words and phrases from Aspects 15-42 of the Arabic text of the book, *Aspects of the Days of Ignorance*.

السَّادِسَةَ عَشْرَةَ: اعْتِيَاضُهُمْ عَمَّا أَتَاهُمْ مِنَ اللهِ بِكُتُبِ السِّحْرِ، كَمَا ذَكَرَ اللهُ ذَلِكَ فِي قَوْلِهِ: ﴿ نَبَذَ فَرِيقٌ مِّنَ ٱلَّذِينَ أُوتُواْ ٱلْكِتَٰبَ كِتَٰبَ ٱللَّهِ وَرَآءَ ظُهُورِهِمْ كَأَنَّهُمْ لَا يَعْلَمُونَ ۝ وَٱتَّبَعُواْ _____ ﴾ [البقرة].

التَّاسِعَةَ عَشْرَةَ: _____،
كَقَدْحِ اليَهُودِ فِي عِيسَى، وَقَدْحِ _____.

الثَّالِثَةُ وَالعِشْرُونَ: أَنَّ الحَيَاةَ الدُّنْيَا غَرَّتْهُمْ، فَظَنُّوا _____، كَقَوْلِهِمْ: ﴿ _____ ﴾ [سبأ: ٣٥].

الخَامِسَةُ وَالعِشْرُونَ: الاِسْتِدْلَالُ عَلَى بُطْلَانِهِ بِسَبْقِ الضُّعَفَاءِ كَقَوْلِهِ: ﴿ _____ _____ ﴾ [الأحقاف: ١١].

التَّاسِعَةُ وَالعِشْرُونَ: أَنَّهُمْ مَعَ ذَلِكَ لَا يَعْمَلُونَ بِمَا تَقُولُهُ طَائِفَتُهُمْ كَمَا نَبَّهَ اللهُ تَعَالَى عَلَيْهِ بِقَوْلِهِ: ﴿ _____ ﴾ [البقرة: ٩١].

157

الحَادِيَةُ وَالثَّلَاثُونَ: وَهِيَ مِنْ أَعْجَبِ الآيَاتِ أَيْضًا، _____

_____، وَمَحَبَّتُهُمْ دِينَ الكُفَّارِ الَّذِينَ عَادَوْهُمْ وَعَادَوْا نَبِيَّهُمْ وَفِتْنَتَهُمْ غَايَةَ

المَحَبَّةِ، كَمَا فَعَلُوا مَعَ _____

وَاتَّبَعُوا كُتُبَ السِّحْرِ، _____.

الرَّابِعَةُ وَالثَّلَاثُونَ: أَنَّ كُلَّ فِرْقَةٍ تَدَّعِي أَنَّهَا النَّاجِيَةُ، فَأَكْذَبَهُمُ اللهُ بِقَوْلِهِ: ﴿ _____

_____ ﴾ [البقرة: ١١١]، ثُمَّ بَيَّنَ الصَّوَابَ بِقَوْلِهِ:

﴿ _____ ﴾ [البقرة: ١١٢].

الحَادِيَةُ وَالأَرْبَعُونَ: نِسْبَةُ النَّقَائِصِ إِلَيْهِ سُبْحَانَهُ، _____

_____.

Fill in the missing words and phrases from Aspects 43-67 of the Arabic text of the book, *Aspects of the Days of Ignorance*.

الثَّالِثَةُ _____ : جُحُودُ _____ .

_____ وَالأَرْبَعُونَ: _____ عَلَى اللهِ بِهِ.

_____ : مُعَارَضَةُ _____ _____ بِقَدَرِهِ.

الثَّالِثَةُ وَالـخَمْسُونَ: إِعْمَالُ الـحِيَلِ _____ ،

كَقَوْلِهِ تَعَالَـى: ﴿ وَمَكَرُواْ وَمَكَرَ ٱللَّهُ ﴾ [آل عمران: ٥٤]، وَقَوْلِهِ: ﴿وَقَالَت طَّآئِفَةٌ مِّنْ

أَهْلِ ٱلْكِتَـٰبِ _____ ﴾ [آل عمران: ٧٢].

الرَّابِعَةُ وَالـخَمْسُونَ: الإِقْرَارُ بِالـحَقِّ _____ .

السَّادِسَةُ وَالـــخَمْسُونَ: تَسْمِيَةُ اتِّبَاعِ الإِسْلَامِ شِرْكًا، كَمَا ذَكَرَهُ فِـي قَوْلِهِ تَعَالَـى:

﴿ مَا كَانَ لِبَشَرٍ _____

_____ ﴾، الآيَةَ [آل عمران: ٧٩].

السَّابِعَةُ _____ : تَحْرِيفُ الكَلِمِ _____ _____ _____ .

_____ والخَمْسُونَ: _____ الأَلْسِنَةِ بِالكِتَابِ.

_____ _____ : تَلْقِيبُ أَهْلِ الهُدَى _____ _____

الثَّانِيَةُ والسِّتُّونَ: كَوْنُهُمْ إِذَا غُلِبُوا بِالحُجَّةِ _____ ، كَمَا قَالُوا:

﴿ _____ ﴾ [الأعراف: ١٢٧].

السَّادِسَةُ والسِّتُّونَ: رَمْيُهُمْ إِيَّاهُمْ بِتَبْدِيلِ الدِّينِ، كَمَا قَالَ تَعَالَى: ﴿ _____

_____ ﴾ [غافر: ٢٦].

_____ _____ : رَمْيُهُمْ إِيَّاهُمْ بِانْتِقَاصِ المَلِكِ، كَقَوْلِهِمْ:

﴿ _____ ﴾ [الأعراف: ١٢٧].

Fill in the missing words and phrases from Aspects 68-113 of the Arabic text of the book, *Aspects of the Days of Ignorance*.

التَّاسِعَةُ وَالسِّتُّونَ: الزِّيَادَةُ فِي العِبَادَةِ، كَفِعْلِهِمْ _____ _____ _____.

_____: نَقْصُهُمْ مِنْهَا، _____ _____ _____ _____.

_____: تَرْكُهُمُ الوَاجِبَ _____ _____.

الثَّانِيَةُ وَالسَّبْعُونَ: تَعَبُّدُهُمْ بِتَرْكِ _____ _____ _____.

السَّـــابِعَةُ وَالسَّـــبْعُونَ: أَنَّ أَئِمَّتَهُمْ إِمَّا _____ _____ _____ _____، وَإِمَّا _____

_____، كَمَا فِي قَوْلِهِ: ﴿ _____ ﴾،

إِلَى قَوْلِهِ: ﴿ _____ ﴾ [البقرة: ٧٥–٧٨].

الخَامِسَةُ وَ _____ وَالثَّمَانُونَ: التَّبَرُّكُ بِآثَارِ المُعَظَّمِينَ، _____ _____ _____،

وَافْتِخَارُ مَنْ كَانَتْ تَحْتَ يَدِهِ بِذَلِكَ، كَمَا قِيلَ لِـ _____ بْنِ _____: بِعْتَ

مَكْرَمَةَ قُرَيْشٍ؟! فَقَالَ: _____.

التَّاسِعَةُ وَالثَّمَانُونَ: الاسْتِسْقَاءُ بِالأَنْوَاءِ.

_____: _____ عَلَى المَيِّتِ.

161

_____ _____ _____: أَنَّ مِنْ دِينِهِم أَخْذَ الرَّجُلِ بِجَرِيمَةِ غَيْرِهِ، فَأَنْزَلَ اللهُ:

﷽ _____ [الأنعام: ١٦٤].

الخَامِسَةُ وَالتِّسْعُونَ: _____ _____ _____ بِمَا فِي غَيْرِهِ، فَقَالَ:

«_____ _____؟!».

السَّادِسَةُ _____: الاِفْتِخَارُ بِوَلَايَةٍ _____، فَذَمَّهُمُ اللهُ بِقَوْلِهِ:

﷽ _____ [المؤمنون: ٦٧].

_____: ازْدِرَاءُ الفُقَرَاءِ، فَأَتَاهُمُ اللهُ بِقَوْلِهِ: ﷽ _____

_____ ﷽ [الأنعام: ٥٢].

الثَّانِيَةُ بَعْدَ المِائَةِ: رَمْيُهُمْ أَتْبَاعَ الرُّسُلِ بِعَدَمِ الإِخْلَاصِ _____ _____ _____،

فَأَجَابَهُمْ بِقَوْلِهِ: ﷽ _____ ﷽، الآيَةَ [الأنعام: ٥٢]، وَأَمْثَالَهَا.

التَّاسِعَةُ بَعْدَ _____: التَّكْذِيبُ بِبَعْضِ مَا أَخْبَرَتْ بِهِ الرُّسُلُ عَنِ اليَوْمِ الآخِرِ، كَمَا

فِي قَوْلِهِ: ﷽ _____ [الكهف: ١٠٥]...

العَاشِرَةُ بَعْدَ المِائَةِ: قَتْلُ _____.

Fill in the missing words and phrases from Aspects 114-128 of the Arabic text of the book, *Aspects of the Days of Ignorance*.

الخَامِسَةَ عَشْرَةَ بَعْدَ المِائَةِ: قَاعِدَةُ الضَّلَالِ، وَهِيَ

_____ .

السَّادِسَةَ عَشْرَةَ بَعْدَ المِائَةِ: التَّنَاقُضُ الوَاضِحُ لَمَّا كَذَّبُوا بِالحَقِّ، كَمَا قَالَ تَعَالَى:

﴿ _____ ﴾ [ق: ٥].

التَّاسِعَةَ عَشْرَةَ بَعْدَ المِائَةِ: مُخَاصَمَتُهُمْ فِيمَا لَيْسَ لَهُمْ بِهِ عِلْمٌ.

_____ دَعْوَاهُمُ اتِّبَاعَ السَّلَفِ _____ .

_____ بَعْدَ المِائَةِ: صَدُّهُمْ _____ .

الثَّالِثَةُ وَالعِشْرُونَ بَعْدَ المِائَةِ، وَالرَّابِعَةُ، وَالخَامِسَةُ، وَالسَّادِسَةُ، وَالسَّابِعَةُ، وَالثَّامِنَةُ وَالعِشْرُونَ بَعْدَ الـمِائَةِ: العِيَافَةُ، وَ _____ ، وَالطِّيَرَةُ، وَ _____ ، وَالتَّحَاكُمُ إِلَى الطَّاغُوتِ، وَ _____ .

163

APPENDIX XIII

CHECK YOUR MEMORIZATION OF THE ENTIRE TEXT

Fill in the missing words and phrases from the Arabic text of the book, *Aspects of the Days of Ignorance*.

فَأَهَمُّ مَا فِيهَا وَأَشَدُّهَا خَطَرًا: _____، فَإِنِ
انْضَافَ إِلَى ذَلِكَ اسْتِحْسَانُ مَا عَلَيْهِ أَهْلُ الْجَاهِلِيَّةِ، _____، كَمَا قَالَ
تَعَالَى: ﴿ _____ ﴾ [العنكبوت: ٥٢].

الثَّانِيَةُ: أَنَّـهُمْ مُتَفَرِّقُونَ _____، كَمَا قَالَ تَعَالَى: ﴿ _____
_____ ﴾ [الروم: ٣٢]، وَكَذَلِكَ فِي دُنْيَاهُمْ، وَيَرَوْنَ _____
_____، فَأَتَى بِالِاجْتِمَاعِ فِي الدِّينِ بِقَوْلِهِ: ﴿ شَرَعَ لَكُم مِّنَ ٱلدِّينِ
﴿ _____
[الشورى: ١٣]، وَقَالَ تَعَالَى: ﴿ _____ ﴾ لَّسْتَ مِنْهُمْ فِي
شَيْءٍ ﴾ [الأنعام: ١٥٩]. وَنَـهَانَا عَنْ مُشَابَـهَتِهِمْ بِقَوْلِهِ: ﴿ _____
_____ ﴾ [آل عمران: ١٠٥]، وَنَهَانَا عَنِ التَّفَرُّقِ فِي الدِّينِ بِقَوْلِهِ:
﴿ وَٱعْتَصِمُواْ _____ ﴾ [آل عمران: ١٠٣].

الثَّالِثَةَ عَشْرَةَ: الْغُلُوُّ فِي الْعُلَمَاءِ وَالصَّالِحِينَ، كَقَوْلِهِ: ﴿ _____
_____ ﴾ [النساء: ١٧١].

165

الثَّالِثَةُ والعِشْرُونَ: أَنَّ الحَيَاةَ الدُّنْيَا غَرَّتْهُمْ، فَظَنُّوا _____،
كَقَوْلِهِمْ: ﴿ _____ ﴾ [سبأ: ٣٥].

السَّابِعَةُ والعِشْرُونَ: تَصْنِيفُ الكُتُبِ البَاطِلَةِ و_____، كَقَوْلِهِ:
﴿ _____ ﴾ [البقرة: ٧٩].

الرَّابِعَةُ والثَّلَاثُونَ: أَنَّ كُلَّ فِرْقَةٍ تَدَّعِي _____ _____ _____، فَأَكْذَبَـهُمُ اللهُ بِقَوْلِهِ:
﴿ _____ ﴾ [البقرة: ١١١]، ثُمَّ بَيَّنَ الصَّوَابَ بِقَوْلِهِ:
﴿ _____ ﴾ [البقرة: ١١٢].

____ : _____ _____ الإِلْحَادُ فِي الصِّفَاتِ، كَقَوْلِهِ تَعَالَى: ﴿ _____ _____
﴿ _____ ﴾ [فصلت: ٢٢].

____ : _____ _____ الإِلْحَادُ فِي الأَسْمَاءِ، كَقَوْلِهِ: ﴿ _____ _____
[الرعد: ٣٠].

الأَرْبَعُونَ: التَّعْطِيلُ، كَقَوْلِ _____ _____ .

السَّادِسَةُ والأَرْبَعُونَ: مَسَبَّةُ الدَّهْرِ، كَقَوْلِهِمْ: ﴿ _____
[الجاثية: ٢٤].

____ : _____ _____ إِضَافَةُ نِعَمِ اللهِ إِلَى غَيْرِهِ كَقَوْلِهِ: ﴿ _____ _____
﴿ _____ ﴾ [النحل: ٨٣].

الخَامِسَةُ _____ : التَّعَصُّبُ لِلْمَذْهَبِ، كَقَوْلِهِ تَعَالَى: ﴿ _____

_____ ﴾ [آل عمران: ٧٣].

_____ **وَالخَمْسُونَ**: تَسْمِيَةُ اتِّبَاعِ الإِسْلَامِ شِرْكًا، كَمَا ذَكَرَهُ فِي قَوْلِهِ تَعَالَى:

﴿ مَا كَانَ لِبَشَرٍ _____

_____ ﴾، الآيَةَ [آل عمران: ٧٩].

الثَّامِنَةُ وَالسَّبْعُونَ: دَعْوَاهُمْ مَحَبَّةَ اللهِ مَعَ تَرْكِهِمْ _____ ، فَطَالَبَهُمُ اللهُ بِقَوْلِهِ:

﴿ _____ ﴾ [آل عمران: ٣١].

التَّاسِعَةُ وَالسَّبْعُونَ: تَمَنِّيهِمُ الأَمَانِيَّ الكَاذِبَةَ، كَقَوْلِهِمْ: ﴿ _____

_____ ﴾ [البقرة: ٨٠]، وَقَوْلِهِمْ: ﴿ لَن يَدْخُلَ ٱلْجَنَّةَ _____

_____ ﴾ [البقرة: ١١١].

السَّابِعَةُ وَالثَّمَانُونَ: الفَخْرُ بِالأَحْسَابِ.

_____ : _____ .

_____ : _____ .

_____ : _____ .

الرَّابِعَةُ وَالتِّسْعُونَ: أَنَّ مِنْ دِينِهِمْ أَخْذَ الرَّجُلِ بِجَرِيْمَةِ _____ ، فَأَنْزَلَ اللهُ:

﴿ _____ ﴾ [الأنعام: ١٦٤].

السَّابِعَةُ وَالتِّسْعُونَ: الاِفْتِخَارُ بِكَوْنِهِمْ ذُرِّيَّةَ الأَنْبِيَاءِ، فَأَتَى اللهُ بِقَوْلِهِ:

﴾ _____ ﴿ [البقرة: ١٣٤].

التَّاسِعَةُ وَالتِّسْعُونَ: عَظَمَةُ الدُّنْيَا فِي قُلُوبِهِمْ، كَقَوْلِهِمْ: ﴾ _____

_____ ﴿ [الزخرف: ٣١].

_____: الإِيمَانُ بِالجِبْتِ وَ_____.

الثَّانِيَةَ عَشْرَةَ بَعْدَ المِائَةِ: تَفْضِيلُ دِينٍ _____ عَلَى دِينٍ _____.

العِشْرُونَ بَعْدَ المِائَةِ: دَعْوَاهُمُ اتِّبَاعَ السَّلَفِ مَعَ _____.

_____: صَدُّهُمْ _____.

_____: مَوَدَّتُهُمْ _____.

من أسانيد رسالة ((مسائل الجاهلية))

قال الخطاء الفقير إلى رحمة ربه أبو العباس موسى الطويل الأمريكي ــ عفا الله عنه ــ :

أروي رسالة ((مسائل الجاهلية)) وغيرها من كتب ورسائل الإمام المجدد محمد بن عبدالوهاب التميمي ــ رحمه الله ــ عن عدد من المشايخ السلفيين الأثبات إجازة.

منهم شيخي العلامة يحيى بن عثمان المدرِّس ــ حفظه الله ــ ؛

وهو يرويها عن الشيخ العلامة أحمد بن يحيى النجمي ــ رحمه الله ــ مدبَّجًا؛

كلاهما عن الشيخ العلامة عبدالرحمن بن عبدالحي بن عبدالكبير الكتّاني ابن صاحب ((فهرس الفهارس))؛

عن الشيخ العلامة أبي بكر ابن محمد عارف بن عبدالقادر خوقير المكي (ت١٣٤٩)؛

عن الشيخ العلامة أحمد بن إبراهيم بن عيسى النجدي (ت١٣٢٩)؛

عن الشيخ العلامة عبدالرحمن بن حسن الحفيد (ت١٢٨٥)؛

عن جده الإمام ــ رحمهم الله جميعًا.

وبذلك ــ بفضل الله تعالى ــ قد اتصل إسنادي ثم إسنادُ مَن سمع مني شيئًا من هذه الكتب النافعة والرسائل المفيدة، ولله الحمد، وصلى الله وسلم وبارك على نبينا محمد وعلى آله وصحبه أجمعين.

APPENDIX XV

ANSWER KEYS FOR MULTIPLE CHOICE QUESTIONS

Use the following answer keys to check your answers to the multiple-choice questions found in Appendix II to Appendix VI.

Appendix II: Aspects 1-14	Appendix III: Aspects 15-42	Appendix IV: Aspects 43-67	Appendix V: Aspects 68-113	Appendix VI: Aspects 114-128
1B	1B	1D	1A	1B
2A	2A	2A	2C	2A
3A	3D	3D	3D	3A
4D	4C	4C	4C	4D
5C	5D	5D	5D	5A
6B	6A	6B	6D	
7D	7C	7A	7B	
8B	8B	8D	8A	
9D	9D	9A	9B	
10D	10D	10D	10D	

Appendix VII: Comprehensive				
1D	6C	11D	16C	21C
2B	7C	12D	17A	22D
3C	8A	13A	18D	23B
4B	9D	14B	19B	24C
5B	10A	15D	20B	25D

السَّادِسَةَ عَشْرَةَ بَعْدَ المِائَةِ: التَّنَاقُضُ الوَاضِحُ لَمَّا كَذَّبُوا بِالـحَقِّ، كَمَا قَالَ تَعَالَى: ﴿ بَلْ كَذَّبُواْ بِٱلْحَقِّ لَمَّا جَآءَهُمْ فَهُمْ فِى أَمْرٍ مَّرِيجٍ ﴾ [ق: ٥].

السَّابِعَةَ عَشْرَةَ بَعْدَ المِائَةِ: الإِيمَانُ بِبَعْضِ المُنَزَّلِ دُونَ بَعْضٍ.

الثَّامِنَةَ عَشْرَةَ بَعْدَ المِائَةِ: التَّفْرِيقُ بَيْنَ الرُّسُلِ.

التَّاسِعَةَ عَشْرَةَ بَعْدَ المِائَةِ: مُخَاصَمَتُهُمْ فِيمَا لَيْسَ لَهُمْ بِهِ عِلْمٌ.

العِشْرُونَ بَعْدَ المِائَةِ: دَعْوَاهُمُ اتِّبَاعَ السَّلَفِ مَعَ التَّصْرِيحِ بِمُخَالَفَتِهِمْ.

الحَادِيَةُ وَالعِشْرُونَ بَعْدَ المِائَةِ: صَدُّهُمْ عَنْ سَبِيلِ اللهِ مَنْ آمَنَ بِهِ.

الثَّانِيَةُ وَالعِشْرُونَ بَعْدَ المِائَةِ: مَوَدَّتُهُمُ الكُفْرَ وَالكَافِرِينَ.

الثَّالِثَةُ وَالعِشْرُونَ بَعْدَ الـمِائَةِ، وَالرَّابِعَةُ، وَالـخَامِسَةُ، وَالسَّادِسَةُ، وَالسَّابِعَةُ، وَالثَّامِنَةُ وَالعِشْرُونَ بَعْدَ الـمِائَةِ: العِيَافَةُ، وَالطَّرْقُ، وَالطِّيَرَةُ، وَالكَهَانَةُ، وَالتَّحَاكُمُ إِلَـى الطَّاغُوتِ، وَكَرَاهَةُ التَّزْوِيجِ بَيْنَ العِيدَيْنِ.

وَاللهُ أَعْلَمُ، وَصَلَّى اللهُ عَلَى مُحَمَّدٍ وَعَلَى آلِهِ وَصَحْبِهِ وَسَلَّمَ.

NOTE: This is the end of the complete Arabic text which reads from right to left, beginning on page 184.

الثَّالِثَةُ بَعْدَ المِائَةِ: الكُفْرُ بِالمَلَائِكَةِ.

الرَّابِعَةُ بَعْدَ المِائَةِ: الكُفْرُ بِالرُّسُلِ.

الخَامِسَةُ بَعْدَ المِائَةِ: الكُفْرُ بِالكُتُبِ.

السَّادِسَةُ بَعْدَ المِائَةِ: الإِعْرَاضُ عَمَّا جَاءَ عَنِ اللهِ.

السَّابِعَةُ بَعْدَ المِائَةِ: الكُفْرُ بِاليَوْمِ الآخِرِ.

الثَّامِنَةُ بَعْدَ المِائَةِ: التَّكْذِيبُ بِلِقَاءِ اللهِ.

التَّاسِعَةُ بَعْدَ المِائَةِ: التَّكْذِيبُ بِبَعْضِ مَا أَخْبَرَتْ بِهِ الرُّسُلُ عَنِ اليَوْمِ الآخِرِ، كَمَا فِي قَوْلِهِ: ﴿ أُوْلَٰٓئِكَ ٱلَّذِينَ كَفَرُواْ بِـَٔايَٰتِ رَبِّهِمْ وَلِقَآئِهِۦ ﴾ [الكهف: ١٠٥]، وَمِنْهَا التَّكْذِيبُ بِقَوْلِهِ: ﴿ مَٰلِكِ يَوْمِ ٱلدِّينِ ﴾ [الفاتحة: ٤]، وَقَوْلِهِ: ﴿ لَّا بَيْعٌ فِيهِ وَلَا خُلَّةٌ وَلَا شَفَٰعَةٌ ﴾ [البقرة: ٢٥٤]، وَقَوْلِهِ: ﴿ إِلَّا مَن شَهِدَ بِٱلْحَقِّ وَهُمْ يَعْلَمُونَ ﴾ [الزخرف: ٦٨].

العَاشِرَةُ بَعْدَ المِائَةِ: قَتْلُ الَّذِينَ يَأْمُرُونَ بِالقِسْطِ مِنَ النَّاسِ.

الحَادِيَةَ عَشْرَةَ بَعْدَ المِائَةِ: الإِيمَانُ بِالجِبْتِ وَالطَّاغُوتِ.

الثَّانِيَةَ عَشْرَةَ بَعْدَ المِائَةِ: تَفْضِيلُ دِينِ المُشْرِكِينَ عَلَى دِينِ المُسْلِمِينَ.

الثَّالِثَةَ عَشْرَةَ بَعْدَ المِائَةِ: لَبْسُ الحَقِّ بِالبَاطِلِ.

الرَّابِعَةَ عَشْرَةَ بَعْدَ المِائَةِ: كِتْمَانُ الحَقِّ مَعَ العِلْمِ بِهِ.

الخَامِسَةَ عَشْرَةَ بَعْدَ المِائَةِ: قَاعِدَةُ الضَّلَالِ، وَهِيَ القَوْلُ عَلَى اللهِ بِلَا عِلْمٍ.

الثَّالِثَةُ وَالتِّسْعُونَ: أَنَّ تَعَصُّبَ الإِنْسَانِ لِطَائِفَتِهِ عَلَى الحَقِّ وَالبَاطِلِ أَمْرٌ لَا بُدَّ مِنْهُ عِنْدَهُمْ، فَذَكَرَ اللهُ فِيهِ مَا ذَكَرَ.

الرَّابِعَةُ وَالتِّسْعُونَ: أَنَّ مِنْ دِينِهِمْ أَخْذَ الرَّجُلِ بِجَرِيْمَةِ غَيْرِهِ، فَأَنْزَلَ اللهُ: ﴿ وَلَا تَزِرُ وَازِرَةٌ وِزْرَ أُخْرَىٰ ﴾ [الأنعام: ١٦٤].

الخَامِسَةُ وَالتِّسْعُونَ: تَعْيِيرُ الرَّجُلِ بِمَا فِي غَيْرِهِ، فَقَالَ: «أَعَيَّرْتَهُ بِأُمِّهِ؟! إِنَّكَ امْرُؤٌ فِيْكَ جَاهِلِيَّةٌ.»

السَّادِسَةُ وَالتِّسْعُونَ: الاِفْتِخَارُ بِوَلَايَةِ البَيْتِ، فَذَمَّهُمُ اللهُ بِقَوْلِهِ: ﴿ مُسْتَكْبِرِينَ بِهِۦ سَٰمِرًا تَهْجُرُونَ ﴾ [المؤمنون: ٦٧].

السَّابِعَةُ وَالتِّسْعُونَ: الاِفْتِخَارُ بِكَوْنِهِمْ ذُرِّيَّةَ الأَنْبِيَاءِ، فَأَتَى اللهُ بِقَوْلِهِ: ﴿ تِلْكَ أُمَّةٌ قَدْ خَلَتْ لَهَا مَا كَسَبَتْ ﴾ [البقرة: ١٣٤].

الثَّامِنَةُ وَالتِّسْعُونَ: الاِفْتِخَارُ بِالصَّنَائِعِ، كَفِعْلِ أَهْلِ الرِّحْلَتَيْنِ عَلَى أَهْلِ الحَرْثِ.

التَّاسِعَةُ وَالتِّسْعُونَ: عَظَمَةُ الدُّنْيَا فِي قُلُوبِهِمْ، كَقَوْلِهِمْ: ﴿ لَوْلَا نُزِّلَ هَٰذَا ٱلْقُرْءَانُ عَلَىٰ رَجُلٍ مِّنَ ٱلْقَرْيَتَيْنِ عَظِيمٍ ﴾ [الزخرف: ٣١].

المِائَةُ: التَّحَكُّمُ عَلَى اللهِ، كَمَا فِي الآيَةِ.

الـحَادِيَةُ بَعْدَ الـمِائَةِ: اِزْدِرَاءُ الفُقَرَاءِ، فَأَتَاهُمُ اللهُ بِقَوْلِهِ: ﴿ وَلَا تَطْرُدِ ٱلَّذِينَ يَدْعُونَ رَبَّهُم بِٱلْغَدَوٰةِ وَٱلْعَشِيِّ ﴾ [الأنعام: ٥٢].

الثَّانِيَةُ بَعْدَ الـمِائَةِ: رَمْيُهُمْ أَتْبَاعَ الرُّسُلِ بِعَدَمِ الإِخْلَاصِ وَطَلَبِ الدُّنْيَا، فَأَجَابَـهُمْ بِقَوْلِهِ: ﴿ مَا عَلَيْكَ مِنْ حِسَابِهِم مِّن شَيْءٍ ﴾، الآيَةَ [الأنعام: ٥٢]، وَأَمْثَالَهَا.

التَّاسِعَةُ وَالسَّبْعُونَ: تَمَنِّيهِمُ الأَمَانِيَّ الكَاذِبَةَ، كَقَوْلِهِمْ: ﴿لَن تَمَسَّنَا ٱلنَّارُ إِلَّآ أَيَّامًا مَّعۡدُودَةٗ﴾ [البقرة: ٨٠]، وَقَوْلِهِمْ: ﴿لَن يَدۡخُلَ ٱلۡجَنَّةَ إِلَّا مَن كَانَ هُودًا أَوۡ نَصَٰرَىٰ﴾ [البقرة: ١١١].

الثَّمَانُونَ: اتِّخَاذُ قُبُورِ أَنْبِيَائِهِمْ وَصَالِحِيهِمْ مَسَاجِدَ.

الحَادِيَةُ وَالثَّمَانُونَ: اتِّخَاذُ آثَارِ أَنْبِيَائِهِمْ مَسَاجِدَ، كَمَا ذُكِرَ عَنْ عُمَرَ.

الثَّانِيَةُ وَالثَّمَانُونَ: اتِّخَاذُ السُّرُجِ عَلَى القُبُورِ.

الثَّالِثَةُ وَالثَّمَانُونَ: اتِّخَاذُهَا أَعْيَادًا.

الرَّابِعَةُ وَالثَّمَانُونَ: الذَّبْحُ عِنْدَ القُبُورِ.

الخَامِسَةُ وَالسَّادِسَةُ وَالثَّمَانُونَ: التَّبَرُّكُ بِآثَارِ المُعَظَّمِينَ، كَدَارِ النَّدْوَةِ، وَافْتِخَارُ مَنْ كَانَتْ تَحْتَ يَدِهِ بِذَلِكَ، كَمَا قِيلَ لِحَكِيمِ بْنِ حِزَامٍ: بِعْتَ مَكْرَمَةَ قُرَيْشٍ؟! فَقَالَ: ذَهَبَتِ المَكَارِمُ إِلَّا التَّقْوَى.

السَّابِعَةُ وَالثَّمَانُونَ: الفَخْرُ بِالأَحْسَابِ.

الثَّامِنَةُ وَالثَّمَانُونَ: الطَّعْنُ فِي الأَنْسَابِ.

التَّاسِعَةُ وَالثَّمَانُونَ: الاسْتِسْقَاءُ بِالأَنْوَاءِ.

التِّسْعُونَ: النِّيَاحَةُ عَلَى المَيِّتِ.

الحَادِيَةُ وَالتِّسْعُونَ: أَنَّ أَجَلَّ فَضَائِلِهِمُ البَغْيُ، فَذَكَرَ اللهُ فِيهِ مَا ذَكَرَ.

الثَّانِيَةُ وَالتِّسْعُونَ: أَنَّ أَجَلَّ فَضَائِلِهِمُ الفَخْرُ، وَلَوْ بِحَقٍّ، فَنُهِيَ عَنْهُ.

الثَّامِنَةُ وَالسِّتُّونَ: دَعْوَاهُمُ الْعَمَلَ بِمَا عِنْدَهُمْ مِنَ الْحَقِّ، كَقَوْلِهِمْ: ﴿ نُؤْمِنُ بِمَآ أُنزِلَ عَلَيْنَا ﴾ [البقرة: ٩١]، مَعَ تَرْكِهِمْ إِيَّاهُ.

التَّاسِعَةُ وَالسِّتُّونَ: الزِّيَادَةُ فِي الْعِبَادَةِ، كَفِعْلِهِمْ يَوْمَ عَاشُورَاءَ.

السَّبْعُونَ: نَقْصُهُمْ مِنْهَا، كَتَرْكِهِمُ الْوُقُوفَ بِعَرَفَاتٍ.

الْحَادِيَةُ وَالسَّبْعُونَ: تَرْكُهُمُ الْوَاجِبَ وَرَعًا.

الثَّانِيَةُ وَالسَّبْعُونَ: تَعَبُّدُهُمْ بِتَرْكِ الطَّيِّبَاتِ مِنَ الرِّزْقِ.

الثَّالِثَةُ وَالسَّبْعُونَ: تَعَبُّدُهُمْ بِتَرْكِ زِينَةِ اللهِ.

الرَّابِعَةُ وَالسَّبْعُونَ: دَعْوَتُهُمُ النَّاسَ إِلَى الضَّلَالِ بِغَيْرِ عِلْمٍ.

الْخَامِسَةُ وَالسَّبْعُونَ: دَعْوَتُهُمْ إِيَّاهُمْ إِلَى الْكُفْرِ مَعَ الْعِلْمِ.

السَّادِسَةُ وَالسَّبْعُونَ: الْمَكْرُ الْكُبَّارُ، كَفِعْلِ قَوْمِ نُوحٍ.

السَّابِعَةُ وَالسَّبْعُونَ: أَنَّ أَئِمَّتَهُمْ إِمَّا عَالِمٌ فَاجِرٌ، وَإِمَّا عَابِدٌ جَاهِلٌ، كَمَا فِي قَوْلِهِ: ﴿ وَقَدْ كَانَ فَرِيقٌ مِّنْهُمْ يَسْمَعُونَ كَلَٰمَ ٱللَّهِ ﴾، إِلَى قَوْلِهِ: ﴿ وَمِنْهُمْ أُمِّيُّونَ لَا يَعْلَمُونَ ٱلْكِتَٰبَ إِلَّا أَمَانِيَّ ﴾ [البقرة: ٧٥-٧٨].

الثَّامِنَةُ وَالسَّبْعُونَ: دَعْوَاهُمْ مَحَبَّةَ اللهِ مَعَ تَرْكِهِمْ شَرْعَهُ، فَطَالَبَهُمُ اللهُ بِقَوْلِهِ: ﴿ قُلْ إِن كُنتُمْ تُحِبُّونَ ٱللَّهَ ﴾ [آل عمران: ٣١].

السَّابِعَةُ وَالخَمْسُونَ: تَحْرِيفُ الكَلِمِ عَنْ مَوَاضِعِهِ.

الثَّامِنَةُ وَالخَمْسُونَ: لَيُّ الأَلْسِنَةِ بِالكِتَابِ.

التَّاسِعَةُ وَالخَمْسُونَ: تَلْقِيبُ أَهْلِ الهُدَى بِالصَّائِبَةِ وَالحَشَوِيَّةِ.

السِّتُّونَ: افْتِرَاءُ الكَذِبِ عَلَى اللهِ.

الحَادِيَةُ وَالسِّتُّونَ: التَّكْذِيبُ بِالحَقِّ.

الثَّانِيَةُ وَالسِّتُّونَ: كَوْنُهُمْ إِذَا غُلِبُوا بِالحُجَّةِ فَزِعُوا إِلَى الشَّكْوَى لِلْمُلُوكِ، كَمَا قَالُوا: ﴿ أَتَذَرُ مُوسَىٰ وَقَوْمَهُ لِيُفْسِدُواْ فِى ٱلأَرْضِ ﴾ [الأعراف: ١٢٧].

الثَّالِثَةُ وَالسِّتُّونَ: رَمْيُهُمْ إِيَّاهُمْ بِالفَسَادِ فِي الأَرْضِ، كَمَا فِي الآيَةِ.

الرَّابِعَةُ وَالسِّتُّونَ: رَمْيُهُمْ إِيَّاهُمْ بِانْتِقَاصِ دِينِ المَلِكِ، كَمَا قَالَ تَعَالَى: ﴿ وَيَذَرَكَ وَءَالِهَتَكَ ﴾ [الأعراف: ١٢٧]، وَكَمَا قَالَ تَعَالَى: ﴿ إِنِّى أَخَافُ أَن يُبَدِّلَ دِينَكُمْ ﴾ [غافر: ٢٦].

الخَامِسَةُ وَالسِّتُّونَ: رَمْيُهُمْ إِيَّاهُمْ بِانْتِقَاصِ آلِهَةِ المَلِكِ، كَمَا فِي الآيَةِ.

السَّادِسَةُ وَالسِّتُّونَ: رَمْيُهُمْ إِيَّاهُمْ بِتَبْدِيلِ الدِّينِ، كَمَا قَالَ تَعَالَى: ﴿ إِنِّى أَخَافُ أَن يُبَدِّلَ دِينَكُمْ أَوْ أَن يُظْهِرَ فِى ٱلأَرْضِ ٱلفَسَادَ ﴾ [غافر: ٢٦].

السَّابِعَةُ وَالسِّتُّونَ: رَمْيُهُمْ إِيَّاهُمْ بِانْتِقَاصِ المَلِكِ، كَقَوْلِهِمْ: ﴿ وَيَذَرَكَ وَءَالِهَتَكَ ﴾ [الأعراف: ١٢٧].

السَّادِسَةُ وَالأَرْبَعُونَ: مَسَبَّةُ الدَّهْرِ، كَقَوْلِهِمْ: ﴿ وَمَا يُهْلِكُنَآ إِلَّا ٱلدَّهْرُ ﴾ [الجاثية: ٢٤].

السَّابِعَةُ وَالأَرْبَعُونَ: إِضَافَةُ نِعَمِ الله إِلَـــى غَيْـــرِهِ كَقَوْلِهِ: ﴿ يَعْرِفُونَ نِعْمَتَ ٱللَّهِ ثُمَّ يُنكِرُونَهَا ﴾ [النحل: ٨٣].

الثَّامِنَةُ وَالأَرْبَعُونَ: الكُفْرُ بِآيَاتِ اللهِ.

التَّاسِعَةُ وَالأَرْبَعُونَ: جَحْدُ بَعْضِهَا.

الخَمْسُونَ: قَوْلُهُمْ: ﴿ مَا أَنزَلَ ٱللَّهُ عَلَىٰ بَشَرٍ مِّن شَيْءٍ ﴾ [الأنعام: ٩١].

الحَادِيَةُ وَالخَمْسُونَ: قَوْلُهُمْ فِي القُرْآنِ: ﴿ إِنْ هَٰذَآ إِلَّا قَوْلُ ٱلْبَشَرِ ﴾ [المدثر: ٢٥].

الثَّانِيَةُ وَالخَمْسُونَ: القَدْحُ فِي حِكْمَةِ اللهِ تَعَالَى.

الثَّالِثَةُ وَالخَمْسُونَ: إِعْمَالُ الـحِيَلِ الظَّاهِرَةِ وَالبَاطِنَةِ فِي دَفْعِ مَا جَاءَتْ بِهِ الرُّسُلُ، كَقَوْلِهِ تَعَالَــــى: ﴿ وَمَكَرُواْ وَمَكَرَ ٱللَّهُ ﴾ [آل عمران: ٥٤]، وَقَوْلِهِ: ﴿ وَقَالَت طَّآئِفَةٌ مِّنْ أَهْلِ ٱلْكِتَٰبِ ءَامِنُواْ بِٱلَّذِيَ أُنزِلَ عَلَى ٱلَّذِينَ ءَامَنُواْ وَجْهَ ٱلنَّهَارِ وَٱكْفُرُواْ ءَاخِرَهُ ﴾ [آل عمران: ٧٢].

الرَّابِعَةُ وَالخَمْسُونَ: الإِقْرَارُ بِالحَقِّ لِيَتَوَصَّلُوا بِهِ إِلَى دَفْعِهِ، كَمَا قَالَ فِي الآيَةِ.

الـخَامِسَةُ وَالـخَمْسُونَ: التَّعَصُّبُ لِلمَذْهَبِ، كَقَوْلِهِ تَعَالَى: ﴿ وَلَا تُؤْمِنُواْ إِلَّا لِمَن تَبِعَ دِينَكُمْ ﴾ [آل عمران: ٧٣].

السَّادِسَةُ وَالـخَمْسُونَ: تَسْمِيَةُ اتِّبَاعِ الإِسْلَامِ شِرْكًا، كَمَا ذَكَرَهُ فِي قَوْلِهِ تَعَالَى: ﴿ مَا كَانَ لِبَشَرٍ أَن يُؤْتِيَهُ ٱللَّهُ ٱلْكِتَٰبَ وَٱلْحُكْمَ وَٱلنُّبُوَّةَ ثُمَّ يَقُولَ لِلنَّاسِ كُونُواْ عِبَادًا لِّي مِن دُونِ ٱللَّهِ ﴾، الآيَةَ [آل عمران: ٧٩].

الرَّابِعَةُ وَالثَّلَاثُونَ: أَنَّ كُلَّ فِرْقَةٍ تَدَّعِي أَنَّهَا النَّاجِيَةُ، فَأَكْذَبَهُمُ اللهُ بِقَوْلِهِ: ﴿ هَاتُواْ بُرْهَانَكُمْ إِن كُنتُمْ صَادِقِينَ ﴾ [البقرة: ١١١]، ثُمَّ بَيَّنَ الصَّوَابَ بِقَوْلِهِ: ﴿بَلَىٰ مَنْ أَسْلَمَ وَجْهَهُ لِلّهِ وَهُوَ مُحْسِنٌ ﴾ [البقرة: ١١٢].

الخَامِسَةُ وَالثَّلَاثُونَ: التَّعَبُّدُ بِكَشْفِ العَوْرَاتِ، كَقَوْلِهِ: ﴿ وَإِذَا فَعَلُواْ فَاحِشَةً قَالُواْ وَجَدْنَا عَلَيْهَآ ءَابَآءَنَا وَٱللَّهُ أَمَرَنَا بِهَا﴾ [الأعراف: ٢٨].

السَّادِسَةُ وَالثَّلَاثُونَ: التَّعَبُّدُ بِتَحْرِيمِ الحَلَالِ، كَمَا تَعَبَّدُوا بِالشِّرْكِ.

السَّابِعَةُ وَالثَّلَاثُونَ: التَّعَبُّدُ بِاتِّخَاذِ الأَحْبَارِ وَالرُّهْبَانِ أَرْبَابًا مِنْ دُونِ اللهِ.

الثَّامِنَةُ وَالثَّلَاثُونَ: الإِلْحَادُ فِي الصِّفَاتِ، كَقَوْلِهِ تَعَالَى: ﴿ وَ· ظَنَنتُمْ أَنَّ ٱللَّهَ لَا يَعْلَمُ كَثِيرًا مِّمَّا تَعْمَلُونَ ﴾ [فصلت: ٢٢].

التَّاسِعَةُ وَالثَّلَاثُونَ: الإِلْحَادُ فِي الأَسْمَاءِ، كَقَوْلِهِ: ﴿ وَهُمْ يَكْفُرُونَ بِٱلرَّحْمَٰنِ﴾ [الرعد: ٣٠].

الأَرْبَعُونَ: التَّعْطِيلُ، كَقَوْلِ آلِ فِرْعَوْنَ.

الحَادِيَةُ وَالأَرْبَعُونَ: نِسْبَةُ النَّقَائِصِ إِلَيْهِ سُبْحَانَهُ، كَالوَلَدِ وَالحَاجَةِ وَالتَّعَبِ، مَعَ تَنْزِيهِ رُهْبَانِهِمْ عَنْ بَعْضِ ذَلِكَ.

الثَّانِيَةُ وَالأَرْبَعُونَ: الشِّرْكُ فِي المُلْكِ، كَقَوْلِ المَجُوسِ.

الثَّالِثَةُ وَالأَرْبَعُونَ: جُحُودُ القَدَرِ.

الرَّابِعَةُ وَالأَرْبَعُونَ: الاحْتِجَاجُ عَلَى اللهِ بِهِ.

الخَامِسَةُ وَالأَرْبَعُونَ: مُعَارَضَةُ شَرْعِ اللهِ بِقَدَرِهِ.

السَّادِسَةُ وَالعِشْرُونَ: تَحْرِيفُ كِتَابِ اللهِ مِنْ بَعْدِ مَا عَقَلُوهُ وَهُمْ يَعْلَمُونَ.

السَّابِعَةُ وَالعِشْرُونَ: تَصْنِيفُ الكُتُبِ البَاطِلَةِ وَنِسْبَتُهَا إِلَى اللهِ، كَقَوْلِهِ: ﴿ فَوَيْلٌ لِّلَّذِينَ يَكْتُبُونَ ٱلْكِتَٰبَ بِأَيْدِيهِمْ ثُمَّ يَقُولُونَ هَٰذَا مِنْ عِندِ ٱللَّهِ ﴾ [البقرة: ٧٩].

الثَّامِنَةُ وَالعِشْرُونَ: أَنَّهُمْ لَا يَقْبَلُونَ مِنَ الحَقِّ إِلَّا الَّذِي مَعَ طَائِفَتِهِمْ، كَقَوْلِهِ: ﴿ قَالُوٓا۟ نُؤْمِنُ بِمَآ أُنزِلَ عَلَيْنَا ﴾ [البقرة: ٩١].

التَّاسِعَةُ وَالعِشْرُونَ: أَنَّهُمْ مَعَ ذَلِكَ لَا يَعْمَلُونَ بِمَا تَقُولُهُ طَائِفَتُهُمْ كَمَا نَبَّهَ اللهُ تَعَالَى عَلَيْهِ بِقَوْلِهِ: ﴿ قُلْ فَلِمَ تَقْتُلُونَ أَنۢبِيَآءَ ٱللَّهِ مِن قَبْلُ إِن كُنتُم مُّؤْمِنِينَ ﴾ [البقرة: ٩١].

الثَّلَاثُونَ: وَهِيَ مِنْ عَجَائِبِ آيَاتِ اللهِ أَنَّهُمْ لَمَّا تَرَكُوا وَصِيَّةَ اللهِ بِالِاجْتِمَاعِ، وَارْتَكَبُوا مَا نَهَى اللهُ عَنْهُ مِنَ الِافْتِرَاقِ، صَارَ كُلُّ حِزْبٍ بِمَا لَدَيْهِمْ فَرِحِينَ.

الحَادِيَةُ وَالثَّلَاثُونَ: وَهِيَ مِنْ أَعْجَبِ الآيَاتِ أَيْضًا، مُعَادَاتُهُمُ الدِّينَ الَّذِي انْتَسَبُوا إِلَيْهِ غَايَةَ العَدَاوَةِ، وَمَحَبَّتُهُمْ دِينَ الكُفَّارِ الَّذِينَ عَادَوْهُمْ وَعَادَوْا نَبِيَّهُمْ وَفِئَتَهُمْ غَايَةَ المَحَبَّةِ، كَمَا فَعَلُوا مَعَ النَّبِيِّ صَلَّى اللهُ عَلَيْهِ وَسَلَّمَ لَمَّا أَتَاهُمْ بِدِينِ مُوسَى عَلَيْهِ السَّلَامِ، وَاتَّبَعُوا كُتُبَ السِّحْرِ، وَهِيَ مِنْ دِينِ آلِ فِرْعَوْنَ.

الثَّانِيَةُ وَالثَّلَاثُونَ: كُفْرُهُمْ بِالحَقِّ إِذَا كَانَ مَعَ مَنْ لَا يَهْوَوْنَهُ، كَمَا قَالَ تَعَالَى: ﴿ وَقَالَتِ ٱلْيَهُودُ لَيْسَتِ ٱلنَّصَٰرَىٰ عَلَىٰ شَىْءٍ وَقَالَتِ ٱلنَّصَٰرَىٰ لَيْسَتِ ٱلْيَهُودُ عَلَىٰ شَىْءٍ ﴾ [البقرة: ١١٣].

الثَّالِثَةُ وَالثَّلَاثُونَ: إِنْكَارُهُمْ مَا أَقَرُّوا أَنَّهُ مِنْ دِينِهِمْ، كَمَا فَعَلُوا فِي حَجِّ البَيْتِ، فَقَالَ تَعَالَى: ﴿ وَمَن يَرْغَبُ عَن مِّلَّةِ إِبْرَٰهِۦمَ إِلَّا مَن سَفِهَ نَفْسَهُ ﴾ [البقرة: ١٣٠].

179

السَّادِسَةَ عَشْرَةَ: اعْتِيَاضُهُمْ عَمَّا أَتَاهُمْ مِنَ اللهِ بِكُتُبِ السِّحْرِ، كَمَا ذَكَرَ اللهُ ذَلِكَ فِي قَوْلِهِ: ﴿ نَبَذَ فَرِيقٌ مِّنَ ٱلَّذِينَ أُوتُوا۟ ٱلْكِتَٰبَ كِتَٰبَ ٱللَّهِ وَرَآءَ ظُهُورِهِمْ كَأَنَّهُمْ لَا يَعْلَمُونَ ۝ وَٱتَّبَعُوا۟ مَا تَتْلُوا۟ ٱلشَّيَٰطِينُ عَلَىٰ مُلْكِ سُلَيْمَٰنَ ﴾ [البقرة: ١٠١-١٠٢].

السَّابِعَةَ عَشْرَةَ: نِسْبَةُ بَاطِلِهِمْ إِلَى الْأَنْبِيَاءِ، كَقَوْلِهِ: ﴿ وَمَا كَفَرَ سُلَيْمَٰنُ ﴾ [البقرة: ١٠٢]، وَقَوْلِهِ: ﴿ مَا كَانَ إِبْرَٰهِيمُ يَهُودِيًّا وَلَا نَصْرَانِيًّا ﴾ [آل عمران: ٦٧].

الثَّامِنَةَ عَشْرَةَ: تَنَاقُضُهُمْ فِي الِانْتِسَابِ، يَنْتَسِبُونَ إِلَى إِبْرَاهِيمَ، مَعَ إِظْهَارِهِمْ تَرْكَ اتِّبَاعِهِ.

التَّاسِعَةَ عَشْرَةَ: قَدْحُهُمْ فِي بَعْضِ الصَّالِحِينَ بِفِعْلِ بَعْضِ الْمُنْتَسِبِينَ إِلَيْهِمْ، كَقَدْحِ الْيَهُودِ فِي عِيسَى، وَقَدْحِ الْيَهُودِ وَالنَّصَارَى فِي مُحَمَّدٍ صَلَّى اللهُ عَلَيْهِ وَسَلَّمَ.

الْعِشْرُونَ: اعْتِقَادُهُمْ فِي مَخَارِيقِ السَّحَرَةِ وَأَمْثَالِهِمْ أَنَّهَا مِنْ كَرَامَاتِ الصَّالِحِينَ، وَنِسْبَتُهُ إِلَى الْأَنْبِيَاءِ، كَمَا نَسَبُوهُ لِسُلَيْمَانَ عَلَيْهِ السَّلَامُ.

الْحَادِيَةُ وَالْعِشْرُونَ: تَعَبُّدُهُمْ بِالْمُكَاءِ وَالتَّصْدِيَةِ.

الثَّانِيَةُ وَالْعِشْرُونَ: أَنَّهُمُ اتَّخَذُوا دِينَهُمْ لَهْوًا وَلَعِبًا.

الثَّالِثَةُ وَالْعِشْرُونَ: أَنَّ الْحَيَاةَ الدُّنْيَا غَرَّتْهُمْ، فَظَنُّوا أَنَّ عَطَاءَ اللهِ مِنْهَا يَدُلُّ عَلَى رِضَاهُ، كَقَوْلِهِمْ: ﴿ نَحْنُ أَكْثَرُ أَمْوَٰلًا وَأَوْلَٰدًا وَمَا نَحْنُ بِمُعَذَّبِينَ ﴾ [سبأ: ٣٥].

الرَّابِعَةُ وَالْعِشْرُونَ: تَرْكُ الدُّخُولِ فِي الْحَقِّ إِذَا سَبَقَهُمْ إِلَيْهِ الضُّعَفَاءُ تَكَبُّرًا وَأَنَفَةً، فَأَنْزَلَ اللهُ تَعَالَى: ﴿ وَلَا تَطْرُدِ ٱلَّذِينَ يَدْعُونَ رَبَّهُم ﴾، الْآيَاتِ [الأنعام: ٥٢].

الْخَامِسَةُ وَالْعِشْرُونَ: الِاسْتِدْلَالُ عَلَى بُطْلَانِهِ بِسَبْقِ الضُّعَفَاءِ كَقَوْلِهِ: ﴿ لَوْ كَانَ خَيْرًا مَّا سَبَقُونَآ إِلَيْهِ ﴾ [الأحقاف: ١١].

التَّاسِعَةُ: الِاقْتِدَاءُ بِفَسَقَةِ الْعُلَمَاءِ، فَأَتَى بِقَوْلِهِ: ﴿ يَـٰٓأَيُّهَا ٱلَّذِينَ ءَامَنُوٓا۟ إِنَّ كَثِيرًا مِّنَ ٱلْأَحْبَارِ وَٱلرُّهْبَانِ لَيَأْكُلُونَ أَمْوَٰلَ ٱلنَّاسِ بِٱلْبَٰطِلِ وَيَصُدُّونَ عَن سَبِيلِ ٱللَّهِ ﴾ [التوبة: ٣٤]، وَقَوْلِهِ: ﴿ لَا تَغْلُوا۟ فِى دِينِكُمْ غَيْرَ ٱلْحَقِّ وَلَا تَتَّبِعُوٓا۟ أَهْوَآءَ قَوْمٍ قَدْ ضَلُّوا۟ مِن قَبْلُ وَأَضَلُّوا۟ كَثِيرًا وَضَلُّوا۟ عَن سَوَآءِ ٱلسَّبِيلِ ﴾ [المائدة: ٧٧].

الْعَاشِرَةُ: الِاسْتِدْلَالُ عَلَى بُطْلَانِ الدِّينِ بِقِلَّةِ أَفْهَامِ أَهْلِهِ، وَعَدَمِ حِفْظِهِمْ، كَقَوْلِهِمْ: ﴿ بَادِىَ ٱلرَّأْىِ ﴾ [هود: ٢٧].

الْحَادِيَةَ عَشْرَةَ: الِاسْتِدْلَالُ بِالقِيَاسِ الفَاسِدِ، كَقَوْلِهِمْ: ﴿ إِنْ أَنتُمْ إِلَّا بَشَرٌ مِّثْلُنَا ﴾ [إبراهيم: ١٠].

الثَّانِيَةَ عَشْرَةَ: إِنْكَارُ القِيَاسِ الصَّحِيحِ، وَالجَامِعُ لِـهَذَا وَمَا قَبْلَهُ عَدَمُ فَهْمِ الجَامِعِ وَالفَارِقِ.

الثَّالِثَةَ عَشْرَةَ: الغُلُوُّ فِي العُلَمَاءِ وَالصَّالِحِينَ، كَقَوْلِهِ: ﴿ يَـٰٓأَهْلَ ٱلْكِتَـٰبِ لَا تَغْلُوا۟ فِى دِينِكُمْ وَلَا تَقُولُوا۟ عَلَى ٱللَّهِ إِلَّا ٱلْحَقَّ ﴾ [النساء: ١٧١].

الرَّابِعَةَ عَشْرَةَ: أَنَّ كُلَّ مَا تَقَدَّمَ مَبْنِيٌّ عَلَى قَاعِدَةٍ وَهِيَ النَّفْيُ وَالإِثْبَاتُ، فَيَتَّبِعُونَ الـهَوَى وَالظَّنَّ، وَيُعْرِضُونَ عَمَّا جَاءَتْ بِهِ الرُّسُلُ.

الـخَامِسَةَ عَشْرَةَ: اعْتِذَارُهُمْ عَنِ اتِّبَاعِ مَا آتَاهُمُ اللهُ بِعَدَمِ الفَهْمِ، كَقَوْلِهِ: ﴿ وَقَالُوا۟ قُلُوبُنَا غُلْفٌ ﴾ [البقرة: ٨٨]، ﴿ يَـٰشُعَيْبُ مَا نَفْقَهُ كَثِيرًا مِّمَّا تَقُولُ ﴾ [هود: ٩١]، فَأَكْذَبَـهُمُ اللهُ، وَبَيَّنَ أَنَّ ذَلِكَ بِسَبَبِ الطَّبْعِ عَلَى قُلُوبِهِمْ، وَأَنَّ الطَّبْعَ بِسَبَبِ كُفْرِهِمْ.

الرَّابِعَةُ: أَنَّ دِينَهُمْ مَبْنِيٌّ عَلَى أُصُولٍ أَعْظَمُهَا التَّقْلِيدُ، فَهُوَ القَاعِدَةُ الكُبْرَى لِـجَمِيعِ الكُفَّارِ أَوَّلِـهِمْ وَآخِرِهِمْ، كَمَا قَالَ تَعَالَى: ﴿ وَكَذَٰلِكَ مَآ أَرْسَلْنَا مِن قَبْلِكَ فِي قَرْيَةٍ مِّن نَّذِيرٍ إِلَّا قَالَ مُتْرَفُوهَآ إِنَّا وَجَدْنَآ ءَابَآءَنَا عَلَىٰٓ أُمَّةٍ وَإِنَّا عَلَىٰٓ ءَاثَٰرِهِم مُّقْتَدُونَ ﴾ [الزخرف: ٢٣]، وَقَالَ تَعَالَى: ﴿ وَإِذَا قِيلَ لَهُمُ ٱتَّبِعُوا مَآ أَنزَلَ ٱللَّهُ قَالُوا بَلْ نَتَّبِعُ مَا وَجَدْنَا عَلَيْهِ ءَابَآءَنَآ أَوَلَوْ كَانَ ٱلشَّيْطَٰنُ يَدْعُوهُمْ إِلَىٰ عَذَابِ ٱلسَّعِيرِ ﴾ [لقمان: ٢١]، فَأَتَاهُمْ بِقَوْلِهِ: ﴿ قُلْ إِنَّمَآ أَعِظُكُم بِوَٰحِدَةٍ أَن تَقُومُوا لِلَّهِ مَثْنَىٰ وَفُرَٰدَىٰ ثُمَّ تَتَفَكَّرُوا مَا بِصَاحِبِكُم مِّن جِنَّةٍ ﴾، الآيَةَ [سبأ: ٤٦]، وَقَوْلِهِ: ﴿ ٱتَّبِعُوا مَآ أُنزِلَ إِلَيْكُم مِّن رَّبِّكُمْ وَلَا تَتَّبِعُوا مِن دُونِهِۦٓ أَوْلِيَآءَ قَلِيلًا مَّا تَذَكَّرُونَ ﴾ [الأعراف: ٣].

الـخَامِسَةُ: أَنَّ مِنْ أَكْبَرِ قَوَاعِدِهِمُ الاغْتِرَارَ بِالأَكْثَرِ، وَيَحْتَجُّونَ بِهِ عَلَى صِحَّةِ الشَّيْءِ، وَيَسْتَدِلُّونَ عَلَى بُطْلَانِ الشَّيْءِ بِغُرْبَتِهِ، وَقِلَّةِ أَهْلِهِ، فَأَتَاهُمْ بِضِدِّ ذَلِكَ، وَأَوْضَحَهُ فِي غَيْرِ مَوْضِعٍ مِنَ القُرْآنِ.

السَّادِسَةُ: الاحْتِجَاجُ بِالـمُتَقَدِّمِينَ، كَقَوْلِهِ: ﴿ قَالَ فَمَا بَالُ ٱلْقُرُونِ ٱلْأُولَىٰ ﴾ [طه: ٥١]، ﴿ مَّا سَمِعْنَا بِهَٰذَا فِي ءَابَآئِنَا ٱلْأَوَّلِينَ ﴾ [المؤمنين: ٢٤].

السَّابِعَةُ: الاسْتِدْلَالُ بِقَوْمٍ أُعْطُوا قُوًى فِي الأَفْهَامِ وَالأَعْمَالِ، وَفِي الـمُلْكِ وَالمَالِ وَالجَاهِ، فَرَدَّ اللهُ ذَلِكَ بِقَوْلِهِ: ﴿ وَلَقَدْ مَكَّنَّٰهُمْ فِيمَآ إِن مَّكَّنَّٰكُمْ فِيهِ ﴾ [الأحقاف: ٢٦]، وَقَوْلِهِ: ﴿ وَكَانُوا مِن قَبْلُ يَسْتَفْتِحُونَ عَلَى ٱلَّذِينَ كَفَرُوا فَلَمَّا جَآءَهُم مَّا عَرَفُوا كَفَرُوا بِهِۦ ﴾ [البقرة: ٨٩]، وَقَوْلِهِ: ﴿ يَعْرِفُونَهُۥ كَمَا يَعْرِفُونَ أَبْنَآءَهُمُ ﴾ [البقرة: ١٤٦].

الثَّامِنَةُ: الاسْتِدْلَالُ عَلَى بُطْلَانِ الشَّيْءِ بِأَنَّهُ لَـمْ يَتَّبِعْهُ إِلَّا الضُّعَفَاءُ، كَقَوْلِهِ: ﴿ قَالُوٓا أَنُؤْمِنُ لَكَ وَٱتَّبَعَكَ ٱلْأَرْذَلُونَ ﴾ [الشعراء: ١١١]، وَقَوْلِهِ: ﴿ أَهَٰٓؤُلَآءِ مَنَّ ٱللَّهُ عَلَيْهِم مِّنۢ بَيْنِنَآ ﴾، فَرَدَّهُ اللهُ بِقَوْلِهِ: ﴿ أَلَيْسَ ٱللَّهُ بِأَعْلَمَ بِٱلشَّٰكِرِينَ ﴾ [الأنعام: ٥٣].

وَهَذِهِ هِيَ الْمَسْأَلَةُ الَّتِي تَفَرَّقَ النَّاسُ لِأَجْلِهَا بَيْنَ مُسْلِمٍ وَكَافِرٍ، وَعِنْدَهَا وَقَعَتِ الْعَدَاوَةُ، وَلِأَجْلِهَا شُرِعَ الْجِهَادُ، كَمَا قَالَ تَعَالَى: ﴿ وَقَٰتِلُوهُمْ حَتَّىٰ لَا تَكُونَ فِتْنَةٌ وَيَكُونَ ٱلدِّينُ كُلُّهُۥ لِلَّهِ ﴾ [الأنفال: ٣٩].

الثَّانِيَةُ: أَنَّهُمْ مُتَفَرِّقُونَ فِي دِينِهِمْ، كَمَا قَالَ تَعَالَى: ﴿ كُلُّ حِزْبٍ بِمَا لَدَيْهِمْ فَرِحُونَ ﴾ [الروم: ٣٢]، وَكَذَلِكَ فِي دُنْيَاهُمْ، وَيَرَوْنَ أَنَّ ذَلِكَ هُوَ الصَّوَابُ، فَأَتَى بِالِاجْتِمَاعِ فِي الدِّينِ بِقَوْلِهِ: ﴿ شَرَعَ لَكُم مِّنَ ٱلدِّينِ مَا وَصَّىٰ بِهِۦ نُوحًا وَٱلَّذِىٓ أَوْحَيْنَآ إِلَيْكَ وَمَا وَصَّيْنَا بِهِۦٓ إِبْرَٰهِيمَ وَمُوسَىٰ وَعِيسَىٰٓ أَنْ أَقِيمُوا۟ ٱلدِّينَ وَلَا تَتَفَرَّقُوا۟ فِيهِ ﴾ [الشورى: ١٣]، وَقَالَ تَعَالَى: ﴿ إِنَّ ٱلَّذِينَ فَرَّقُوا۟ دِينَهُمْ وَكَانُوا۟ شِيَعًا لَّسْتَ مِنْهُمْ فِي شَىْءٍ ﴾ [الأنعام: ١٥٩].

وَنَهَانَا عَنْ مُشَابَهَتِهِمْ بِقَوْلِهِ: ﴿ وَلَا تَكُونُوا۟ كَٱلَّذِينَ تَفَرَّقُوا۟ وَٱخْتَلَفُوا۟ مِنۢ بَعْدِ مَا جَآءَهُمُ ٱلْبَيِّنَٰتُ ﴾ [آل عمران: ١٠٥]، وَنَهَانَا عَنِ التَّفَرُّقِ فِي الدِّينِ بِقَوْلِهِ: ﴿ وَٱعْتَصِمُوا۟ بِحَبْلِ ٱللَّهِ جَمِيعًا وَلَا تَفَرَّقُوا۟ ﴾ [آل عمران: ١٠٣].

الثَّالِثَةُ: أَنَّ مُخَالَفَةَ وَلِيِّ الْأَمْرِ وَعَدَمَ الِانْقِيَادِ لَهُ فَضِيلَةٌ، وَالسَّمْعَ وَالطَّاعَةَ لَهُ ذُلٌّ وَمَهَانَةٌ، فَخَالَفَهُمْ رَسُولُ اللهِ صَلَّى اللهُ عَلَيْهِ وَسَلَّمَ، وَأَمَرَ بِالصَّبْرِ عَلَى جَوْرِ الْوُلَاةِ، وَأَمَرَ بِالسَّمْعِ وَالطَّاعَةِ لَهُمْ وَالنَّصِيحَةِ، وَغَلَّظَ فِي ذَلِكَ، وَأَبْدَى فِيهِ وَأَعَادَ.

وَهَذِهِ الْمَسَائِلُ الثَّلَاثُ هِيَ الَّتِي جَمَعَ بَيْنَهَا فِيمَا صَحَّ عَنْهُ صَلَّى اللهُ عَلَيْهِ وَسَلَّمَ فِي الصَّحِيحَيْنِ أَنَّهُ قَالَ: «إِنَّ اللهَ يَرْضَى لَكُمْ ثَلَاثًا: أَنْ تَعْبُدُوهُ، وَلَا تُشْرِكُوا بِهِ شَيْئًا، وَأَنْ تَعْتَصِمُوا بِحَبْلِ اللهِ جَمِيعًا وَلَا تَفَرَّقُوا، وَأَنْ تُنَاصِحُوا مَنْ وَلَّاهُ اللهُ أَمْرَكُمْ»، وَلَمْ يَقَعْ خَلَلٌ فِي دِينِ النَّاسِ وَدُنْيَاهُمْ إِلَّا بِسَبَبِ الْإِخْلَالِ فِي هَذِهِ الثَّلَاثِ أَوْ بَعْضِهَا.

APPENDIX XVI
COMPLETE VOWELED TEXT OF THE BOOK

بِسْمِ اللهِ الرَّحْمَنِ الرَّحِيمِ

هَذِهِ أُمُورٌ خَالَفَ فِيهَا رَسُولُ اللهِ صَلَّى اللهُ عَلَيْهِ وَسَلَّمَ أَهْلَ الْـجَاهِلِيَّةِ الْكِتَابِيِّينَ وَالْأُمِّيِّينَ، مِمَّا لَا غِنَى لِلْمُسْلِمِ عَنْ مَعْرِفَتِه.

فَالضِّدُّ يُظْهِرُ حُسْنَهُ الضِّدُّ   وَبِضِدِّهَا تَتَبَيَّنُ الْأَشْيَاءُ

فَأَهَمُّ مَا فِيهَا وَأَشَدُّهَا خَطَرًا: عَدَمُ إِيمَانِ الْقَلْبِ بِمَا جَاءَ بِهِ الرَّسُولُ صَلَّى اللهُ عَلَيْهِ وَسَلَّمَ، فَإِنِ انْضَافَ إِلَـى ذَلِكَ اسْتِحْسَانُ مَا عَلَيْهِ أَهْلُ الْـجَاهِلِيَّةِ، تَـمَّتِ الْـخَسَارَةُ، كَمَا قَالَ تَعَالَـى: ﴿ وَالَّذِينَ ءَامَنُوا۟ بِالْبَاطِلِ وَكَفَرُوا۟ بِٱللَّهِ أُو۟لَٰٓئِكَ هُمُ ٱلْخَاسِرُونَ ﴾ [العنكبوت: ٥٢].

الْـمَسْأَلَةُ الْأُولَى: أَنَّهُمْ يَتَعَبَّدُونَ بِإِشْرَاكِ الصَّالِـحِينَ فِي دُعَاءِ اللهِ وَعِبَادَتِهِ، يُرِيدُونَ شَفَاعَتَهُمْ عِنْدَ اللهِ لِظَنِّهِمْ أَنَّ اللهَ يُحِبُّ ذَلِكَ، وَأَنَّ الصَّالِـحِينَ يُحِبُّونَهُ، كَمَا قَالَ تَعَالَى: ﴿ وَيَعْبُدُونَ مِن دُونِ ٱللَّهِ مَا لَا يَضُرُّهُمْ وَلَا يَنفَعُهُمْ وَيَقُولُونَ هَٰٓؤُلَآءِ شُفَعَٰٓؤُنَا عِندَ ٱللَّهِ ﴾ [يونس: ١٨]، وَقَالَ تَعَالَى: ﴿ وَالَّذِينَ ٱتَّخَذُوا۟ مِن دُونِهِۦٓ أَوْلِيَآءَ مَا نَعْبُدُهُمْ إِلَّا لِيُقَرِّبُونَآ إِلَى ٱللَّهِ زُلْفَىٰٓ ﴾ [الزمر: ٣].

وَهَذِهِ أَعْظَمُ مَسْأَلَةٍ خَالَفَهُمْ فِيهَا رَسُولُ اللهِ صَلَّى اللهُ عَلَيْهِ وَسَلَّمَ، فَأَتَى بِالْإِخْلَاصِ، وَأَخْبَرَ أَنَّهُ دِينُ اللهِ الَّذِي أَرْسَلَ بِهِ جَمِيعَ الرُّسُلِ، وَأَنَّهُ لَا يُقْبَلُ مِنَ الْأَعْمَالِ إِلَّا الْخَالِصُ، وَأَخْبَرَ أَنَّ مَنْ فَعَلَ مَا اسْتَحْسَنُوا فَقَدْ حَرَّمَ اللهُ عَلَيْهِ الْجَنَّةَ وَمَأْوَاهُ النَّارُ.

Made in the USA
Columbia, SC
08 December 2019